LAS VEGAS
and
LAUGHLIN, NEVADA

Automobile Club of Southern California

Cover photo:
The Egyptian-themed Luxor Las Vegas hotel-casino.

ISBN: 1-56413-460-1
Printed in the United States of America

© 1999 by the Automobile Club of Southern California
Member Information and Communication Services A327
3333 Fairview Road, Costa Mesa, California 92626

Table of Contents

LAS VEGAS & LAUGHLIN, NEVADA

Southern Nevada is a land of extremes and contrasts: mega-resorts and huge dams, the spectacle of bizarre rock formations and the din of gambling halls, dressed-up showgirls and fuzzy burros, thrill rides and wedding chapels.... People love it and hate it, sometimes all at once. But from the barren desert to the most elaborate casinos and hotels, Southern Nevada and all its offerings cannot be ignored.

Las Vegas is one of the nation's favorite vacation destinations. It's a 24-hour city where gambling reigns supreme and dreams of striking it rich sometimes come true. But Las Vegas has many facets, and casino action is just one of them. It also offers luxurious resort lodgings, top-name entertainment, inexpensive dining, world-class golf courses, scenic desert treks, nearby water recreation, and most recently, plenty of activities for children. Las Vegas is home to nine of the 10 largest resort hotels in the world—top of the list being the 5005-room MGM Grand Hotel Casino & Theme Park. Not surprisingly, there are also more hotel rooms here than any other city in the U.S.: 105,000, with thousands more on the way. In 1997, Las Vegas attracted an estimated 31 million visitors, up more than 5 percent from 1996 and a figure that just seems to keep growing.

Laughlin, by contrast, offers a more relaxed atmosphere than its flashy northern counterpart. It is an oasis along the Colorado River, where the state lines of California, Nevada and Arizona merge. Like Las Vegas, Laughlin offers plenty of gaming action, but the river remains one of its strongest assets. The area, which generally includes adjacent **Bullhead City, Arizona**, has long been known as a haven for "snowbirds" in winter (travelers from cold climes who migrate during the winter to the sun-belt states) and the river crowd in summer. Boating, fishing, water-skiing and swimming in the river's surprisingly frigid waters are favorite pursuits of vacationers, especially during the sizzling heat of summer. Combine the lure of the river with reasonably priced rooms, countless buffets, and even an international airport, and it should be

Theme hotels dominate the new Las Vegas Strip.

Laughlin has become a boomtown on the banks of the Colorado River.

no surprise that Laughlin has gained such a foothold in the West. In 1996, more than 4.6 million tourists visited this small desert community.

*A*nother town quickly making a name for itself is **Primm**, located along I-15, 40 miles south of Las Vegas at the California-Nevada border. Once just a meager drive-through known as Stateline, the settlement now boasts one of the world's tallest and fastest roller coasters, the "Desperado," and is the site of three large resort-style hotels, a 6500-seat arena, a monorail and various other attractions.

Climate

Las Vegas experiences about 294 days of sunshine per year and an average high temperature of 79 degrees Fahrenheit. This high desert community has an arid climate, low humidity and a yearly rainfall of about 4 inches. Spring and fall generally bring the mildest weather, when daytime highs are in the comfortable 70-degree range. Winter months, by contrast, can be quite cool, with highs in the 50s and lows in the 30s.

At the peak of summer, the temperature often climbs above 100 degrees. But the heat is easily escaped via air conditioning, swimming pools or jaunts to water parks. Scenic Mount Charleston in the Spring Mountains National Recreation Area also offers a break from the heat with its cooler upper-elevation temperatures.

Laughlin is located on the northeast edge of the Mojave Desert and has a high mean temperature of about 87 degrees. In this hot, dry region, the summer months routinely sizzle above the 100-degree mark, sometimes climbing above 120 degrees. But relief is always close at hand in the form of air conditioning and the frigid water of the Colorado River. Sometimes higher-than-average humidity triggers summer thunderstorms and flash floods, turning the area's dry washes into turbulent rivers. Winters can be equally severe with below-freezing temperatures. Rainfall averages about 4 inches a year.

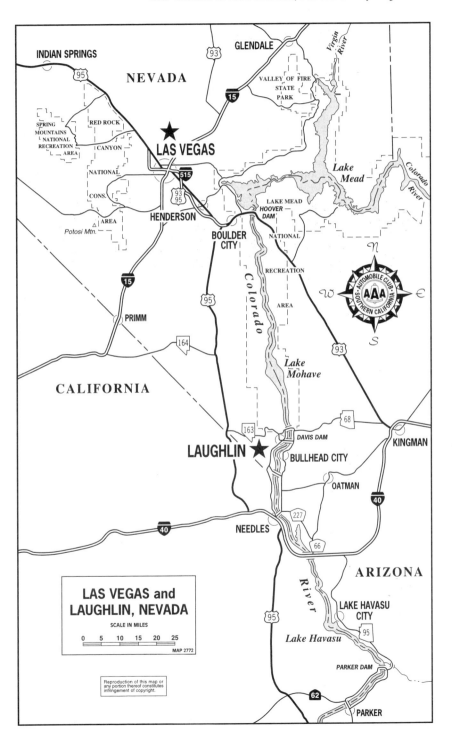

▼ *Showing the Way*

To guide travelers through the area's varied and sometimes staggering array of attractions, the Automobile Club of Southern California created this book as a reference to the many activities, points of interest and places to stay in Las Vegas, Laughlin and surrounding areas. In addition to *Las Vegas and Laughlin, Nevada*, the Auto Club produces a number of companion publications. The *Guide to Colorado River* covers the river area from Lake Mead to Yuma, and provides thorough map coverage and information on recreation and local attractions. Publications covering nearby areas include the *Explore! San Bernardino County* map, which offers a recreation guide, listings for points of interest and detailed maps. These publications are available to AAA members at Auto Club district offices, as well as to nonmembers at selected Central and Southern California booksellers.

Activities For Children

Because Las Vegas and Laughlin are usually considered adult-oriented cities, visitors in the past have often left children at home. Today, however, both desert communities offer many daytime diversions for the younger set. Nearly all of the larger hotels have some form of entertainment for children, and some even offer supervised children's programs.

In Las Vegas, supervised children's programs can be found at the Orleans, Gold Coast Hotel and the MGM Grand. These programs allow adults the freedom to investigate the more mature attractions, while the children do whatever it is that children do. These facilities typically offer arts and crafts, video games, jungle gyms, puzzles and group play activities. Basketball, table tennis,

pool and even food service are available at some facilities. The MGM Grand has the unique opportunity to offer children guided tours of the hotel's theme park, when it is in operation. This outdoor attraction features roller coasters and water rides, bumper cars and musical acts. Admission requirements vary from facility to facility and may include age limitations, independent toileting skills, a limit on how long a child may stay and a requirement that the parents stay on the property. Parents should call about reservations and fees. Additional child-care services in Las Vegas may be found by referring to the telephone directory yellow pages under "Baby Sitters."

While the day care is strictly for children, Las Vegas' many other youth-oriented attractions will entertain both the child and adult. These activities can be loosely organized into three different categories: those that augment a hotel's ability to attract patrons, stand-alone entertainment or information facilities, and less commercial outdoor-style activities.

The resort-sponsored activities are designed to attract and entertain families. The Circus Circus Hotel, for example, has several shops and food stands catering to children, while the second floor boasts a carnival-style arcade and free circus acts. Circus Circus also has the Adventuredome, a five-acre, climate-controlled indoor amusement park. The attractions include a water flume ride with a 60-foot free-fall and the nation's only double-loop, double-corkscrew indoor roller coaster. The Excalibur Hotel delights young children with its medieval castle-themed exterior and Renaissance village interior. Strolling performers, carnival-style arcade games and a nightly jousting tournament can all be found here. The Excalibur also has Merlin's Magic Motion Machine, a dynamic motion simulator that provides filmed "rides" for passengers whose seats are programmed to move with the motion on the screen. For a tropical

Rafting on the Colorado River is just one of many recreational activities available in the Las Vegas region.

beach-inspired Las Vegas vacation, island hoppers will be happy to find Mandalay Bay. This resort's 11-acre water park provides areas for sunning, body-boarding as well as sandcastle-building.

Children will be awestruck with the sites and activities available to them at the Mirage, Treasure Island and the Bellagio. A spectacular five-story waterfall and volcano are located at the entrance to The Mirage. Every night the manmade volcano erupts in a dramatic fashion, spewing fire and smoke—and stopping traffic on Las Vegas Boulevard. Dramatic night lighting makes the waterfall appear to be flowing lava. Inside the hotel, children will enjoy the Dolphin and Secret Garden Habitat or the white tiger display. Treasure Island, next to The Mirage, features a spectacular pirate show several times nightly. Swashbucklers battle it out right in front of the hotel on Las Vegas Boulevard. Dazzling, fiery explosions and even the sinking of a ship provide exciting entertainment for all ages. At the entrance to the Bellagio is an 8½-acre lake that features a fountain show every 30 minutes each afternoon and evening. The

Bellagio's Gallery of Fine Art exhibits works from the Impressionism movement. Period works from 1870 to 1970 are on display.

If imitation is the greatest form of flattery, then Las Vegas has nothing but accolades for Egypt, New York, Venice and Paris. Of particular interest to children are the Luxor and New York New York. The latter resort is boastful of its' namesake, while the Luxor is an Egyptian-themed resort. Its pyramid shape is the most salient feature among an eclectic mix of Egyptian replicas, including an enormous sphinx in front and a full-size reproduction of King Tut's tomb. Other enticing distractions are a video arcade and a series of motion-simulated films. Equally impressive is Las Vegas' rendition of the East Coast—New York New York's Coney Island Emporium features midway-style carnival games; laser tag; an eight-player, Daytona-style, interactive driving simulator; bumper cars; shooting galleries and more. Next door to the emporium is the Manhattan Express roller coaster, nearly a mile in length with a maximum drop of 144 feet.

The 1950s-themed shop at the Everything Coca-Cola store sells merchandise celebrating the venerable soft drink.

zoo, miniature train rides and staged gunfights at Bonnie Springs Old Nevada. Only 45 minutes from Las Vegas is Spring Mountains National Recreation Area (part of Humboldt-Toiyabe National Forest), where mountain scenery, cooler temperatures and, in season, snow-skiing can be found.

Lake Mead National Recreation Area, 20 miles east of Las Vegas, has year-round fishing, swimming, hiking and picnicking, as well as guided tours of magnificent Hoover Dam. Children might also be interested to see American Indian petroglyphs in Grapevine Canyon, the local artifacts at the Colorado River Museum, or a close-up look at Davis Dam. There are also plenty of opportunities for hiking, fishing and swimming; Davis Camp County Park is an excellent place for all three. (See listings in the *Laughlin-Bullhead City* chapter.) Las Vegas also has many stand-alone, non-gaming entertainment facilities. GameWorks is a huge virtual-reality arcade, with almost 300 video games of all description. The centerpiece is Surge Rock, at 75 feet one of the world's tallest freestanding rock-climbing structures. Crowds gather to watch climbers of all ages try their luck at scaling the earthtone rock. Other venues for young people include the Guinness World of Records Museum, Imperial Palace Auto Collection, Las Vegas Natural History Museum, Las Vegas Mini Grand Prix, Lied Discovery Children's Museum, Magic & Movie Hall of Fame, Nevada State Museum and Historical Society, Scandia Family Fun Center, Southern Nevada Zoological-Botanical Park, Wet 'n Wild and World of Coca-Cola. Details about these attractions can be found in the *Las Vegas Valley, Outside Las Vegas* and *Laughlin-Bullhead City* chapters.

For those who find neon unappealing or wagering wasteful, there are destinations in and around Las Vegas that are not commercially saturated. Oatman, for example, is an Old West mining town that will prove to be a treat for all ages. The relaxed atmosphere is personified by a group of friendly but wild burros that roam the streets, often greeting visitors in hopes of a snack (carrots are sold at local stores). Entertaining gunfights are staged on weekends and holidays, and the town is fraught with small antique and souvenir shops that may be of interest to older children.

Other less commercial attractions include Valley of Fire State Park and Red Rock Canyon National Conservation Area. These natural resources offer dramatic views of towering rust-colored sandstone formations, and abundant opportunities for hiking and picnicking. A few miles from Red Rock Canyon, children will especially enjoy the petting

Other children's activities can be found in Primm and Henderson. Visitors to Primm will find the "Desperado" roller coaster and other thrill rides, while Henderson touts the Cranberry World West, Ethel M Chocolates Factory, Ron Lee's World of Clowns and Favorite Brands Marshmallow Factory.

While Laughlin's orientation toward gambling is mostly for adults, parents will find plenty of activities to entertain their children in and around the gambling center.

The Colorado Belle, Edgewater, Flamingo Hilton, Gold River, Harrah's Laughlin, Pioneer, Ramada Express and Riverside hotels all have video arcades.

First-run movies are shown at Don Laughlin's Riverside Resort Hotel and at theaters in Bullhead City. Boat trips on the Colorado River offer both fresh air and adventure, and auto enthusiasts should definitely make time to see the exotic cars at Don Laughlin's Classic Car Collection

The Ramada Express has a narrow-gauge railroad with a steam locomotive that takes passengers for a ride around the parking lot. The train consists of an engine and two open-air passenger cars, which have a combined capacity of 65 passengers. The rides are free and the train operates daily. Inside the hotel there is also a play area for young children that features a train.

Friendly engineers and conductors take passengers around the parking lot on a narrow-gauge train at the Ramada Express Hotel in Laughlin.

▼ *Tipping*

A tip, or gratuity, for services rendered is customary in Las Vegas, as it is in any U.S. city. Although entirely at the customer's discretion, prompt, friendly and good quality service traditionally merits a tip. In Las Vegas and Laughlin, there is an especially staggering array of service personnel—all who supplement their income with tips—including card dealers, slot people, showroom maitre d's and pool attendants. When in doubt about the amount, 15 to 20 percent of the total bill is usually appropriate. Following are some helpful guidelines:

Bartenders/Cocktail Servers—For parties of two to four people, a tip of $1 per round is standard; more for larger groups.

Bell Captains, Bellmen, Skycaps—Luggage is usually tipped at $1-2 per bag or around $5 if you have several bags. If you plan on using the concierge or VIP services for arrangements for shows, travel or car, a $5 tip is appropriate.

Child Care Attendants—Baby-sitting is no easy task, so a tip of $2-5 for two to four hours of child-care service is appreciated.

Dealers—It is customary make a small bet for the dealer or tip a chip when you are winning.

Hotel Maids—A tip upon departure of $1 per day is appreciated.

Lounge Attendants—Approximately 50¢ to $1 in the attendant's tray is appropriate for being handed towels, soap, etc.

Masseuse/Masseur—The 15- to 20-percent rule is standard.

Pool Attendants—Fifty cents to $1 is customary for towels, pads, lounges, etc.

Showroom Maitre d's—For unassigned restaurant-style seating, it is customary to tip the maitre d' from $5-10 to improve location—up to $20 or more for the really big acts. No tips are required at shows with assigned seating.

Slot People/Keno Runners—A $1 tip now and then is appropriate for good service from keno runners and slot people.

Taxi Drivers—A tip of $1-2 for a direct route is expected, more if the driver is friendly and helps with the door and your luggage.

Tour Guides—A tip of $1-2 per person at the end of the trip is suggested.

Valet Parking Attendants—A tip of $1-2 is standard.

Waiters/Room Service—The 15- to 20-percent rule applies for both. With room service, the tip is sometimes included in the bill; be sure to ask when you place your order.

Shopping

Most of the big resort hotels in Las Vegas and Laughlin have shopping venues. These usually feature a dozen or so stores selling designer fashions, furs, jewelry, artwork, toys and international gifts. One of the largest of these arcades is in Las Vegas at Bally's Casino Resort, which boasts 40 stores. Sam's Town, east of the Strip at Flamingo Road and Boulder Highway in Las Vegas, features a huge Western-wear emporium; its 40,000 square feet of retail space make it one of the largest such stores west of the Rockies. Another large, elaborate mall is The Forum Shops at Caesars, which doubled its size in 1997 to more than half a million square feet; it's perhaps best known for its sky-like ceiling with lighting that changes from "day" to "night" in less than an hour. The Grand Canal Shoppes at the Venetian feature a faux sky-ceiling reproduction of Piazza St. Marco. Other notable shopping centers and factory outlets in Las Vegas include the Boulevard Mall, Chinatown Plaza, Factory Stores of America, Belz Factory Outlet World and the Meadows and Fashion Show malls. (See *Las Vegas Valley* chapter for more detailed listings.)

The larger hotels are also good places to find shops that carry such necessities as aspirin, toothbrushes, film, postage stamps, magazines and other miscellaneous items. These shops are usually centrally located near the front entrance of the hotel, the registration desk or the casino.

In addition to the numerous shopping outlets in Las Vegas, Laughlin boasts the new Horizon Outlet Center at the corner of Casino Drive and Edison Way. The 258,000-square-foot mall features more than 50 food and retail outlets, a movie theater and a basement garage with 1220 parking spaces.

For the real souvenir hound there is also no shortage of trinket shops. Hats, shirts, coffee mugs, salt and pepper shakers, genuine leather purses, Indian dolls, turquoise jewelry, dice, playing cards and poker chips are widely available. In Las Vegas, these shops are mainly along the Strip area of Las Vegas Boulevard from Charleston Boulevard south to Tropicana Avenue. Downtown, they are located one block off Fremont between Main and 4th streets.

The Forum Shops at Caesars Palace offers upscale shopping in a Roman village setting.

History

*Las Vegas is Spanish for "The Fertile Plain," so named for its numerous springs and once verdant landscape. The surrounding harsh and unforgiving Mojave Desert protected this oasis for centuries from all but the native Paiute Indians. It was not until 1829 when the first known inhabitants of European descent settled. By comparison, **Laughlin** is a much more recent arrival, beginning in 1966 with Don Laughlin's aerial view of the area's barren, formidable landscape. From his private plane, the native Midwesterner saw investment potential along a vacant stretch of the Colorado River, next to the then 11-year-old Davis Dam and the sparsely populated town of Bullhead City, Arizona.*

The discovery of abundant spring water at what is now **Las Vegas** shortened the Spanish Trail to Los Angeles, eased the rigors for Spanish traders and hastened the rush west for California gold. Some 14 years later, John C. Frémont, an American soldier and explorer, led an overland expedition west and camped at Las Vegas Springs. Fremont Street and numerous other area landmarks carry his name.

The modern history of Las Vegas began in 1855, when a small group of Mormon settlers arrived. They came to protect the mail route between Los Angeles and Salt Lake City, but for the next three years were also engaged in fruit and vegetable cultivation and lead mining at Potosi Mountain.

The Mormons abandoned their mining activity when the bullets made from their ore proved to be flaky and brittle due to an extremely high silver content—a problem other miners would liked to have had. American Indian raiding parties also added to their problems. The Mormons' 150-square-foot adobe fort was abandoned in 1858; a portion of it can be seen today near the intersection of Las Vegas Boulevard North and Washington Avenue (see Old Las Vegas Mormon Fort State Historic Park in the *Las Vegas Valley* chapter).

In 1864 Nevada was admitted to the Union as the 36th state, although the 11,000 square miles surrounding Las Vegas were part of the Arizona territory. It was not until two years later that Congress ceded the region to Nevada, establishing the current state borders.

Farming and ranching were the main focus of Las Vegas until the coming of the railroad. On May 15, 1905, the Union Pacific Railroad auctioned off 1200 lots in a single day—lots that soon sprouted gambling houses, saloons and stores. In 1910 Nevada passed an anti-gambling law so strict that it even forbade the Western custom of flipping a coin for the price of a drink. Despite the law, which remained in effect for 20 years, gambling continued to flourish in the form of "underground" games, where patrons uttered a secret password to play.

Legalized gambling returned to the state in 1931, at the height of the Great Depression. It was also the same year construction started on the Boulder Canyon Project. Thousands of jobless citizens, victims of the nation's economic slump, streamed into the Las Vegas-Boulder City area for work. At its peak, the project employed 5128 people and had an average monthly payroll of $500,000. In 1935 President Franklin Roosevelt dedicated the structure, known then as "Boulder Dam." In April 1947, by congressional action, the 726-foot-high structure was officially designated Hoover Dam, the name by which it is known today.

Fremont Street (1929) as Las Vegas awaits inspection as a housing center for thousands of Boulder Dam (Hoover Dam) construction workers.

Petroglyphs in Grapevine Canyon (near Laughlin) show evidence of the region's Indian heritage.

The great hydroelectric project on the Colorado River originally brought power to Las Vegas, and this abundant source of electricity helped create the famous neon city. (Today Las Vegas' power primarily comes from coal-burning power stations.) In 1940 a group of Los Angeles investors, speculating on the resort potential of the area, built El Rancho Vegas, the first hotel on what became the Las Vegas Strip. Shortly thereafter, the Last Frontier was completed, followed by the fabulous Flamingo, a hotel and casino built by the infamous mobster Benjamin "Bugsy" Siegel. (Six months after the Flamingo's 1946 opening, Siegel was murdered by an unknown assailant in Beverly Hills, California.)

The momentum established by these early resorts has continued ever since, taking off in the post-World War II years as the town emerged to become a major tourist destination. High-rise hotels with blazing marquees began to rise along a stretch of Las Vegas Boulevard that would soon be known as simply the Strip. The Riviera, Stardust, Hacienda and Dunes were but a few of those to open during the 1950s, and their names soon became familiar far beyond the Nevada state line.

Casino gambling was the main draw at most venues, but entertainment helped seal Las Vegas' reputation as a playground getaway. In 1941, when El Rancho Las Vegas was the only Strip resort, singers, comedians, strippers and other performers entertained guests in its small, intimate showroom.

Other resorts copied that successful format by headlining big-name entertainers of their own. The Stardust blazed a new path in the 1950s when it made a stage-spectacular its main entertainment feature. The hotel imported "Lido de Paris" from France, a critically acclaimed show that enjoyed a 31-year run before being replaced by the present-day production, "Enter the Night." The Tropicana followed suit with another French import when it bought the U.S. rights to the "Folies Bergere" in 1960. It remains a favorite to this day.

Casino lounges emerged as well during the post-war years, offering dusk-to-dawn entertainment while spawning stars like Don Rickles, Buddy Hackett, Alan King and the Mary Kaye Trio. Meanwhile, the famed "Rat Pack" of Frank Sinatra, Dean Martin and Sammy Davis Jr. crooned to hundreds of sellout audiences during their heydays in the 1950s and '60s. Sinatra would remain a star attraction decades later, packing the crowds into the early 1990s.

No one did more for the town's entertainment image, however, than the King himself, Elvis Presley. By 1964, when he romanced Ann-Margaret in the film "Viva Las Vegas," he had established himself as a major Strip attraction, and his greatest glory days still lay ahead. Between 1969 and 1976, Presley performed to more than 1500 sellout crowds at the Las Vegas Hilton, a one-man windfall for the town's tourism business.

While gambling remained the number one lure, in 1976 the town faced competition for the first time when New Jersey voters approved a ballot measure to open casinos in Atlantic City. Las Vegas confronted the challenge by transforming itself to a family-friendly destination. As early as 1968, Circus Circus

Rising like an oasis in the desert is Primm, once a mere border casino and now boasting three hotel-casinos featuring thrill rides and swimming pools, as well as name big-entertainment.

opened on the Strip, with carnival games and midway-style rides beneath its circus tent-shaped roof, but the transformation did not take off until the late 1980s.

When the Mirage opened in 1989, it featured a white tiger habitat, dolphin pool and man-made volcano among its many noncasino attractions. A year later came the Excalibur, a 4000-room property designed like a medieval castle, with jousting knights, court jesters and entire floors devoted to nongambling entertainment. The '90s building frenzy was under way, reaching its peak in late 1993 when three huge properties, the Luxor, Treasure Island and MGM Grand, opened within three months of each other. With 5005 rooms, the MGM Grand became the world's largest hotel property.

While the 1993, 12,000-room, single-year growth has not been eclipsed, growth has far from ebbed. The tide continues to crest, with an eye toward opulence. The 1998 opening of the most expensive hotel property in history, the Bellagio, demonstrated a continued faith in the ability of Las Vegas to attract high rollers. The Bellagio features a gallery with works of art by Monet, van Gogh, Renoir, Matisse and other Impressionist artists. Mandalay Bay Resort and Casino incorporates a tropical theme throughout its property, featuring an 11-acre wave pool, a House of Blues and a Four Seasons hotel.

In a town where bigger has always been better, a new breed of resort is establishing itself. Modeling and miniaturization are their focus. New York, Venice and Paris have been scaled and relocated in a way that could only be Vegas. The Statue of Liberty, Empire State Building and the Chrysler Building re-create the Big Apple's skyline at New York New York. The romantic evenings of Venice have arrived on the strip at the Venetian,

complete with gondoliers plying canals, the *Ca D'Oro* (Palace of Gold), the Bridge of Sighs and even the Rialto Bridge. And if your interests are fashion, Brie and wine, look no further then Paris-Las Vegas, which is scheduled to open in September 1999. The resort will feature a 50-story replica of the Eiffel Tower, where 100 feet above the Strip guests may dine in a gourmet restaurant, or ride a glass elevator to the top where an observation deck provides panoramas of the city.

Population has grown dramatically at the same time, as Las Vegas swelled from 258,000 residents in 1990 to 425,000 by mid-1997. Likewise, Clark County is now home to more than 1.1 million people, compared to 768,000 when the decade began. By some estimates that figure could top 1.5 million by the year 2010.

Perhaps befitting that growth, Las Vegas has never paid great homage to its history, choosing instead to focus on tomorrow. As an example, when the Hilton Corporation tore down an older section of the Flamingo Hotel in 1993, it also razed the fortress-like "Bugsy Suite" with its false stairways and bulletproof office that the famed gangster used before his death. The Flamingo name survives, but each year entire hotels of bygone eras are felled to clear the way for bigger, more elaborate resorts than ever before.

Even when Las Vegas does preserve the past, it reinvents itself in order to adapt to the ever-changing tastes of visitors. Take Fremont Street, the famed "Glitter Gulch," which had lost out years ago to the Strip as the center of gambling and entertainment action. A four-block section of the street was closed to traffic in 1995 and transformed into the Fremont Street Experience, a pedestrian mall crowned by a 90-foot-high canopy with more than 2 million lights. The street now hosts a series of dazzling sound and light shows on the hour every night.

As the 21st century unfolds, water short-falls may slow the region's long-term growth. Most of Las Vegas' water comes from the Colorado River, which Nevada must share with seven other states. If present trends continue, the state will use up its allotment within 10 years, cur-tailing growth if new supplies are not developed.

Before 1966, what is now **Laughlin** was composed of one roadhouse restau-rant at the end of a dirt road. The area was known as South Pointe, the name of a construction camp that housed workers for nearby Davis Dam. (South Pointe's population disappeared follow-ing completion of the dam in 1953.) Entrepreneur Don Laughlin, fresh from a successful 10-year gaming venture in Las Vegas, purchased and renovated the deteriorating restaurant as a casino in 1966, naming it appropriately "Riverside." In 1977 the growing com-munity was officially named after its entrepreneur-founder.

Initially, Laughlin's customers were resi-dents of Bullhead City, enticed by the free ferry service from a parking lot on the Arizona side of the river. As news of the friendly, informal atmosphere of the Riverside Casino got out, people from greater distances showed up. Soon the new business was a great success, which induced Laughlin to expand his opera-tion. Others quickly saw the potential for the gaming business along the shores of the Colorado, so beginning in 1967 with what is now the Golden Nugget (originally called the Bob Cat), addition-al casino/hotels began to rise. Today nine major casinos occupy the west riverbank of the Colorado at Laughlin; another sits a block back from the water, and still another lies nine miles to the south of town on the Fort Mojave Indian Reservation. Those casinos were the main draw to the 4.6 million people who visited Laughlin in 1996.

Across the river in Bullhead City, the boomtown atmosphere is equally intense. Rugged mountains provide a scenic backdrop and contain mines and ghost towns of historic importance. Katherine Mine, Chloride and Oatman give travelers an enticing glimpse into the world of the Wild West. A drive along historic Route 66 through Oatman and Kingman, Arizona, is not only pleasing to the eye, with the area's wonderfully jagged mountaintops, wind-ing roads and alluring vistas, but it serves as a reminder of those who, during the 1930s, migrated from the parched Midwest on this very road, seeking a better life. More than 28,000 people reside in Bullhead City today.

In 1987, Laughlin supplanted Lake Tahoe as Nevada's third-largest gaming resort (after Las Vegas and Reno), and plans for further growth are a major topic of local conversation. Laughlin has clearly come a long way from its humble beginnings, when coyotes outnumbered the town's population. The town's 8500 residents are still outnumbered, however, this time by more than 11,000 slot machines.

Then there's **Primm**, the latest town to make a pitch for the hearts and wallets of visitors to Southern Nevada. Known for years as Stateline, the town changed its name in 1996 to honor Gary Primm, who owned the three hotel-casinos in this outpost at the California state line. Once just a dusty rest stop along I-15, Primm has become a destination in its own right with its modern hotel-casinos, thrill rides and the Primm Valley Golf Club, which opened in 1997.

Casino Games

From 1931 until the mid-1970s, Nevada was the only state that offered legalized gambling. This fact alone helped make Las Vegas the single most popular tourist destination in the United States. The profits from gambling can be enormous, and most efforts to attract new visitors could not be underwritten without the lucrative casinos.

*B*efore embarking on one or more of the many games of chance, it's a good idea to become familiar with a game's rules and strategy. Gambling instruction is offered in most casinos and, in some cases, on the hotel's cable television channel. Understanding the intricacies of a game will not only increase your odds of winning but also make it more enjoyable to play. Do not expect dealers or croupiers to be of much help; they have a job to do and will offer assistance and advice only when they can. A good way to get to know a game is to watch the action for a while before joining in; observation is a cheap way of learning some of the more obvious lessons.

There are many books devoted to the art of casino gambling. These books have complete explanations of the rules, strategy, odds, wagering and systems that claim to give players an advantage. But be skeptical of the systems: statistically they might work in the long run, but few players have the time and the resources to last, or the concentration and mental dexterity that are often required. The serious student will spend some time practicing at home before venturing into a casino to test his or her mettle. And finally, a last piece of advice: Before placing any bets, determine how much you can afford to lose and set that money aside for gambling. Should it cross to the other side of the tables, don't dig for more! It is not just a cliché that people can lose everything they have.

BACCARAT A game very similar to chemin de fer, baccarat (pronounced Ba-Ca-Rah) is played with eight decks of cards dealt from a box called a "shoe." Two cards are given to each of two players, with one player being designated the bank. The object of the game is to come as close to the number nine as possible. All tens and face cards are counted as zero. Other people at the table bet on either the bank or the player.

BINGO Most bingo games in Las Vegas and Laughlin are played on "boards" with three bingo cards on each board. There is both open-play and party bingo at most casinos. In open-play bingo, each board costs between 10¢ and 40¢ per game. Party bingo is played at set hours; cards cost $1 to $4 each with a $3 to $6 minimum; approximately 10 to 12 games are played during each party session.

BLACKJACK Also called "21," blackjack is one of the most popular card games, mainly because it's fast and easy to learn. The object of the game is to beat the dealer by getting as close to 21 as possible without going over that count.

CRAPS By far the most complicated casino game; craps offers literally dozens of different ways to bet on the dice. The action is fast and the amount of money exchanging hands is considerable. Craps is not a good game for the timid, but it's great fun to watch.

KENO This is an adaptation of an ancient Chinese game. Players mark a series of favorite numbers between one and 80 that appear on the blank keno ticket. Twenty numbers are then drawn at random. The amount of money won depends on the type of ticket played and how many winning numbers were selected. Many restaurants and lounges have keno runners who take the bets. Keno is also a popular game to play on slot machines.

PAI GOW This ancient Chinese game involves 32 dominoes that are shuffled by the dealer and then placed in eight stacks of four each. Up to eight players are dealt one stack. The object of the game is to set the four dominoes into two pairs for the best ranking combinations.

PAI GOW POKER This game is a combination of poker and Pai Gow. It is played with an ordinary deck of 52 cards plus one joker. The joker is used as an ace or to complete a straight or flush. Players are dealt seven cards each, which are arranged into two hands. One hand contains five cards and is known as the "high hand," while the other hand has only two cards and is called the "low hand." The object of the game is to win the bet by having both the high and low hands rank higher than the respective hands of the banker. The ranking is determined by traditional poker rules.

POKER The rules are pretty much the same for casino poker as they are for home games, except that the house provides a dealer who manages the game without playing a hand. The house makes money by taking a small

percentage of each pot. Check the rules carefully before sitting down at a game.

RACE AND SPORTS BOOKS Bets can be made on practically any horse race, boxing match, or professional or collegiate game (as long as it does not involve a Nevada event) from the comfort of race and sports books. Live events are shown on giant, satellite-fed screens. Most of the major hotels have race and sports books.

ROULETTE The roulette wheel has 36 numbers plus a green zero and a green double zero. Bets can be made on one number, a group, a color or a column of numbers. Odds on roulette range from 35-to-1 to even money. For example, if the player wins by betting on a single number, he or she is paid $35 for every $1 wagered. This is strictly a game of luck and intuition, so there's no reason to worry about skill level. Low stakes games are common, so a few dollars can keep a player going for quite some time.

SLOT MACHINES One-armed-bandits and video poker comprise the majority of slots, but gamblers will also find video blackjack, video keno and a variety of other games offered. Nickel, quarter and dollar machines are the most prevalent and today most slots don't even require coins or tokens—they accept U.S. bills of many denominations. There are a variety of ways to win, including multiple pay lines, fixed jackpots and progressives (slots linked to statewide networks). To win the big jackpots and progressives requires more than the minimum bet; some machines accept up to 10 bets (or coins) at once.

Marriage Information

In Las Vegas, two words spoken as frequently as "hit me" and "double down" are with-out a doubt, "I do." Where else but in this unique desert community are marriage licenses issued so swiftly (one every 5½ minutes) and Elvis impersonators able to preside over the ceremonies. Seven days a week, 24 hours a day on weekends (correct change required), wedding vows are taken at drive-up windows, on bungee jumping platforms and boats, in helicopters, hotel suites and churches, and at dozens of wedding chapels. Ninety miles to the south, Laughlin now has its own branch of the Clark County Clerk's Office, and couples there can get hitched on the Colorado River aboard Mississippi-style riverboats or in any number of wedding chapels.

Marriages in **Las Vegas** total more than 100,000 per year, due in part to the ease of getting a marriage license. Historically, the most popular wedding day here is February 14 (Valentine's Day), with December 31 (New Year's Eve) running a close second. Among the famous who have married in Las Vegas are Elvis and Priscilla Presley, Frank Sinatra and Mia Farrow, Richard Gere and Cindy Crawford, Paul Newman and Joanne Woodward, and Bruce Willis and Demi Moore.

The "Marriage Capital of the World" weds 100,000 couples each year.

To purchase a marriage license, the bride and groom must simply appear at the Marriage Bureau Office, located in the county courthouse at 200 South 3rd Street, or the Justice Courts in Laughlin or Mesquite. No legal residency is required. Blood tests are not needed and there is no waiting period. Persons can not be nearer of kin than second cousins or cousins of half blood. Persons ages 16 and 17 years of age must have the consent of their parents or legal guardians. Persons giving consent must have proof of identity and guardianship. Proof of age may be required. If the bride or groom was previously married, divorce must be final in the state in which it was granted; no papers are required. The office is open daily; Monday through Thursday from 8 a.m. to midnight, and

continuously (24 hours) from 8 a.m. Friday to midnight Sunday; 24 hours on holidays. The license fee is $35. For information, call the Marriage Bureau Office at (702) 455-4415.

Marriage ceremonies can be performed by the Commissioner of Civil Marriages, 309 South 3rd Street, or in one of the many wedding chapels in town (more than 50 at last count). The commissioner's office charges $35, and the hours are the same as the Marriage Bureau's. Wedding chapel fees depend on the elaborateness of the ceremony. Many of the large hotel/casino complexes have wedding chapels on the grounds. For a list of wedding chapels, see the Las Vegas telephone directory yellow pages under "Wedding."

An additional branch of the Marriage Bureau serves the community of **Laughlin**. Couples wishing to marry in this river city can obtain a license at the Justice Court Office in the Regional Government Center, 101 Civic Way. Licenses are issued Tuesday through Thursday from 8 a.m. to 4:30 p.m., Friday from 8 a.m. to 6 p.m. and Saturday from 10 a.m. to 4 p.m., closed Sunday and Monday. No waiting period or blood test is required. All that is necessary is the $35 license fee in cash and proof of age. The Laughlin-Bullhead City area offers wedding services at several wedding chapels and aboard riverboats. Ceremonies can also be performed in the Justice Court Office (appointments are required). There is an additional $35 recording fee here for a total charge of $70. For more information, call the Justice Court Office at (702) 298-4622. Wedding chapels can be found in the Laughlin-Bullhead City telephone directory yellow pages under "Wedding Chapels and Ceremonies."

Las Vegas Valley

Today's gambling meccas offer an array of activities for the whole family. Contrary to the adults-only atmosphere of the past, **Las Vegas** *now promotes a child-friendly environment that's hard to resist. Roller coasters, water parks, virtual reality theaters, laser shows, and an assortment of museums have sprung up across the city and neighboring communities that comprise the Las Vegas Valley.*

The biggest change, though, has been the 1990s proliferation of huge, meticulously designed hotels. It's no longer enough to boast how many guest rooms you have or how "loose" the casino slots may be; today's properties have adopted elaborate themes throughout to lure visitors their way. Just drive up from the south end of the Strip, where traffic slows to a crawl while drivers shamelessly gawk at the huge pyramid and ½-scale sphinx of the Egyptian-themed Luxor. Next door stands the surreal white castle of the Excalibur, which salutes the legend of King Arthur. Just beyond that soars the third-scale Manhattan skyline of New York New York, paying homage to its namesake city. Farther up, snarling pirates and gallant sailors wage battle nightly in front of Treasure Island.

With hotels often filled to capacity, the continued growth in and around Las Vegas seems to be unlimited. Without a doubt, audacious creativity, unabashed flamboyance and a dash of irreverence have proved a winning formula in wooing more and more visitors to modern-day Las Vegas.

POINTS OF INTEREST

Attractions are listed alphabetically by city or area—**Henderson**, **Las Vegas** and **North Las Vegas**. Listings connected to hotel properties do not imply AAA endorsement for the lodging establishment.

Henderson

See **A Quick Guide to Las Vegas** in this chapter under Las Vegas.

CLARK COUNTY HERITAGE MUSEUM *13 miles southeast of Las Vegas at 1830 S. Boulder Hwy. (US 93/95), 89015. (702) 455-7955. Open daily 9 a.m.-4:30 p.m. Closed Jan. 1 and Dec. 25. Adults, $1.50; ages 55 and over and 3-15, $1.* This 25-acre museum houses regional memorabilia, historic structures and artifacts. Heritage Street's collection of six historic homes and commercial buildings includes many which have been fully restored to reflect the lifestyles of their respective eras. Other outdoor exhibits include authentic rolling stock, mining equipment and a "ghost town" comprised of

several structures dating to the 1880s. The 8000-square-foot indoor Exhibit Center features special theme displays, and a permanent Southern Nevada timeline exhibit that dates from prehistoric times to the present.

Authentic rolling stock is exhibited at the Clark County Heritage Museum.

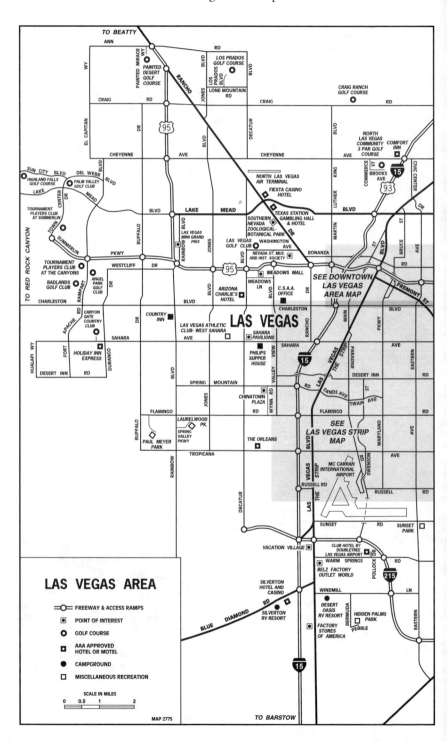

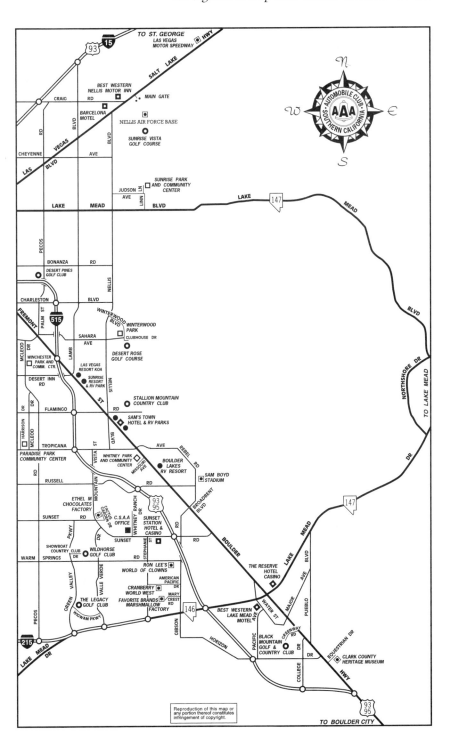

CRANBERRY WORLD WEST *Off Gibson Rd. at 1301 American Pacific Dr., 89014. (702) 566-7160, (800) 289-0917. Open daily 9 a.m.-5 p.m.; call for holiday hours. Free.* The Ocean Spray Visitor Center is the site of this self-guided tour, adjacent to the Henderson processing plant. The tour begins with a six-minute film explaining the history and processing of the cranberry, then offers a glimpse into the bottling operations and a series of interactive exhibits geared to children. At the end of the tour, the demonstration kitchen provides free samples of juice drinks and a variety of cranberry-inspired treats. The gift shop offers a number of gourmet and novelty items for sale.

ETHEL M CHOCOLATES FACTORY *8 miles southeast of the Strip, off Sunset Wy.; 2 Cactus Garden Dr., 89014. Recorded information (702) 433-2500. Open daily 8:30 a.m.-7 p.m. Closed Thanksgiving and Dec. 25. Free.* Ethel M's self-guided tour offers a behind-the-scenes look at the ingredients and machinery used in the candy-making process. Adjacent to the factory is a 2½-acre cactus garden. At the end of the tour, participants get a chance to sample their favorite Ethel M chocolate and shop for more tempting treats in the gift store.

FAVORITE BRANDS MARSHMALLOW FACTORY *Off Gibson and Mary Crest rds.; 1180 Marshmallow Ln., 89014. (702) 564-3878. Open daily 9 a.m.-4:30 p.m. Closed Sun. and major holidays. It is recommended that you call before hand to insure that the factory is*

Chocoholics will crave a visit to the Ethel M Chocolates Factory.

in production. Free. This self-guided tour offers visitors a chance to view the entire marshmallow-making process from start to finish. A free bag of marshmallows is given to each visitor at the end of the tour. T-shirts and marshmallow treats can be purchased in the gift shop.

RON LEE'S WORLD OF CLOWNS
Off Gibson and Warm Springs rds.; 330 Carousel Pkwy., 89014. (702) 434-1700. Open Mon.-Sat. 9 a.m.-5 p.m. Closed Sun. and major holidays. Free tour; carousel rides, $1. The mold-making and painting processes of clown and animation figurines are shown during this self-guided tour. Through windows, visitors see the artisans at work; a video at each station explains the process being done. A large gift shop features the final products for sale, and a gourmet cafe offers sandwiches, salads, pastries, coffee and more. The facility also houses a 30-foot Chance Carousel—a favorite with children.

Las Vegas

THE ADVENTUREDOME—*See Circus Circus Hotel & Casino.*

A.J. HACKETT BUNGEE *Adjacent to Circus Circus Hotel & Casino; 810 Circus Circus Dr., 89109. (702) 385-4321. Open daily; May through Sep., 10 a.m.-midnight; Oct. through Apr., Mon.-Fri. 11 a.m.-9 p.m., Sat.-Sun. 11 a.m.-11 p.m. $49 per person; additional jumps same day, $20 per person.* This New Zealand-based company has several locations around the world and a record of more than 1 million incident-free jumps. Participants plunge 171 feet from North America's highest double platform over a 12-foot pool. Video and T-shirt packages available.

BELLAGIO *3600 Las Vegas Boulevard S, 89109. (888) 987-6667.*

The Bellagio Gallery of Fine Art
Daily 8 a.m.-11:30 a.m. $10 admission; reservations 7 days in advance for local guests; 90 days for out of town guests. Wheelchair accessible. Twenty-five works of art including sculptures and paintings will be on display and rotated from various collections. The gallery focuses on the Impressionist Movement of the 1870s and contemporary artists. Works by Monet, van Gogh, Renoir, Matisse, de Kooning and Lichtenstein are all part of the rotating collections.

The Fountains of Bellagio *Shows every half hour from 2 p.m.-midnight.* A choreographed fountain show takes place on the 8½-acre lake entrance to the Bellagio. Shows are announced with the chiming of bells in the nearby campanile.

▼ Show Your Card and Save

Certain attractions offer AAA members a special discount. The discount is given to both adults and children, and applies to the member and his or her family traveling together, usually up to six persons. The discount may not apply if any other gate reduction is offered or if tickets are purchased through an agent rather than at the attraction's ticket office. Because attractions offering such discounts change frequently, they are not listed here. For current information on such discounts, check the most recent edition of the AAA *California/Nevada TourBook*. When in doubt, ask if a discount is available at the time of your visit.

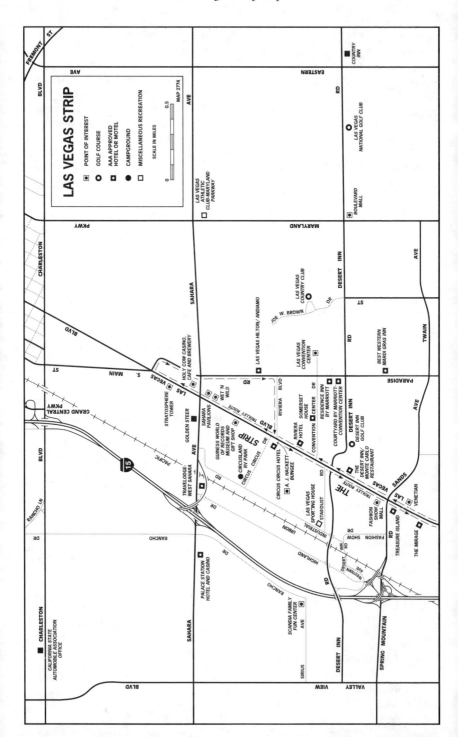

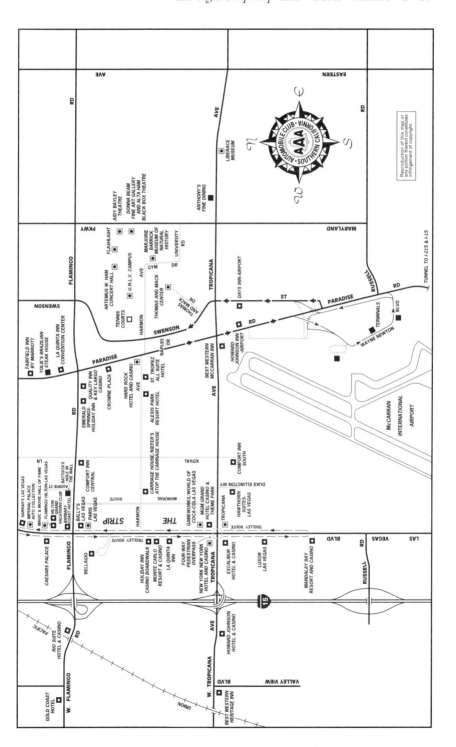

BELZ FACTORY OUTLET WORLD *Corner of Las Vegas Blvd. S. and Warm Springs Rd.; 7400 Las Vegas Blvd. S., 89123. (702) 896-5599. Open daily at 10 a.m.; Mon.-Sat. to 9 p.m., Sun. to 6 p.m. Smoke-free building.* This 600,000-square-foot indoor mall has 159 outlets and a carousel.

BOULEVARD MALL *Maryland Pkwy. and Desert Inn Rd.; 3528 S. Maryland Pkwy., 89109. (702) 732-8949. Open daily; Mon.-Fri. 10 a.m.-9 p.m., Sat. 10 a.m.-8 p.m., Sun. 11 a.m.-6 p.m. Closed Easter, Thanksgiving and Dec. 25.* This 1 million-square-foot indoor mall is among the largest shopping centers in Nevada.

BUCCANEER BAY—*See Treasure Island.*

CAESARS PALACE *3750 Las Vegas Blvd. S., 89109. (702) 731-7110.*

Caesars Magical Empire *Dinner shows daily 4:30-11 p.m. $75-200; discount for early and late seating. Tours daily 11 a.m.-4 p.m. Free.* Magic, mystery and dining converge in this attraction, where visitors are entertained before and during their meals. Greeters dressed as Roman sentries lead guests to one of 10 dining chambers or two séance rooms, where a magician takes charge and performs an array of mystical feats during dinner. Tours of the dining/entertainment complex, including a "Lumineria" show with dancing, fire, smoke and lighting effects, are available during pre-dining hours.

The Forum Shops *Open daily at 10 a.m.; Sun.-Thu. to 11 p.m., Fri.-Sat. to midnight.* This upscale indoor mall features a Roman motif, talking statues and a domed "sky" that changes colors. A 1997 expansion doubled the mall's size to 533,000 square feet, with a total of more than 110 shops and restaurants. The centerpiece of the expansion is a hall 160 feet in diameter with an 85-foot-high ceiling, featuring a display called "Atlantis" that features animated figures.

Omninax Theatre *Open daily; showings every 70 minutes Sun.-Thu. 2 p.m.-10:10 p.m., Fri.-Sat. 11:40 a.m.-10:10 p.m.; programs change regularly. Adults, $7; ages 55 and over, military and ages 2-12, $5.* The 368-seat theater projects movies on a super-sized screen. Seats recline to a 27-degree angle, allowing the audience an unparalleled view of the screen. The theater has a six-track stereophonic sound system with 16 speaker banks and 86 individual speakers.

CASHMAN CENTER *North of downtown; 850 Las Vegas Blvd. N., 89101. (702) 386-7100.* The center contains two large exhibition halls, a 1954-seat theater and a 10,000-seat baseball field. The Las Vegas Stars professional baseball club of the Pacific Coast League play at this location from early April through September.

CHINATOWN PLAZA *West of the Strip; 4255 Spring Mountain Rd., 89102. (702) 221-8448, 222-0590. Open daily; store hours vary.* This shopping plaza has more than two dozen specialty shops that carry jewelry, handcrafted furniture, clothing and other merchandise from the Orient. In addition to several restaurants, one of the largest Oriental supermarkets in Nevada is located here.

▼ *A Quick Guide to Las Vegas and Vicinity*

Population
405,254 (City of Las Vegas)
1,136,782 (Clark County)

Elevation   2174 ft.

Emergency   911

Police (nonemergency)

Boulder City   (702) 293-9224
Henderson   (702) 565-8933
Metropolitan Las Vegas, Mount
Charleston and North Las Vegas
                      (702) 649-9111

Highway Conditions
                      (702) 486-3116

Time   (702) 844-1212

Weather

Las Vegas   (702) 248-4800
Mount Charleston, Lake Mead
                      (702) 736-3854

Emergency Road Service for AAA Members

(800) AAA-HELP (in the USA and
Canada)
(800) 955-4TDD (for the hearing
impaired)

Newspapers

The major daily newspapers are the
Las Vegas Review Journal and the *Las
Vegas Sun*. The biweekly publication
What's On In Las Vegas, distributed
in hotels, motels and other tourist
venues, provides information on local
attractions, dining and entertainment.

Radio Stations

Christian: KILA (90.5 FM), KKVV
(1060 AM); **Classic Rock:** KKLZ
(96.3 FM), KOMP (92.3 FM), KXTE
(107.5 FM); **Contemporary/Rock:**
KCEP (88.1 FM), KLUC (98.5 FM),
KMZQ (100.5 FM), KSNE (106.5
FM), KXPT (97.1 FM), KMXB (94.1
FM); **Country:** KFMS (102 FM),
KIXW (101.5/107.3 FM), KWNR
(95.5 FM); **Highway News:** KHWY
(98.5 FM); **Jazz:** KUNV (91.5 FM);
News/Sports/Talk: KDWN (720
AM), KENO (1460 AM), KLAV
(1230 AM), KORK (920 AM),
KVBC (105.1 FM), KNXT (840
AM), KNEWS (970 AM); **Oldies:**
KBGO (93.1 FM), KOOL (105.5
FM); **Public Radio/Classical:** KNPR
(89.5 FM); **Spanish:** KDOL (1280
AM). For a complete list of radio pro-
grams, consult the daily newspapers.

TV Stations

The area's major television stations
include channels 3 (NBC), 5 (FOX),
8 (CBS), 10 (PBS), 13 (ABC), 21
(UPN), 33 (WB) and 39 (Spanish).
For a complete list of television programs, consult the daily newspapers.

Public Transportation

The **Downtown Transportation
Center,** located at Stewart Ave. and
Casino Center Blvd., serves as a
transportation hub for Citizens Area
Transit (CAT) buses and the downtown trolley. Most bus lines connect
to the center, as does the trolley system. The center is open daily; Mon.-
Fri. 6 a.m.-10 p.m.; Sat., Sun. and
holidays 6 a.m.-6 p.m. In addition to
ticket and route information personnel, the facility also has a restaurant.

Bus *(702) 228-7433. One-way fares
for routes 301, 302 and 303: adults,*

$1.50; ages 62 and over, 5-17 and persons with disabilities, 50¢. One-way fares for all other routes: adults, $1; ages 62 and over, 5-17 and persons with disabilities, 50¢. **Exact change is required.** *Tokens (called CAT Coins) or a monthly pass can be purchased at the Downtown Transportation Center.* One easy way to travel from place to place on the Strip, or between the Strip and downtown, is to take the CAT bus. Daily from 5 a.m. to midnight, the CAT bus (Route 301) runs at 10-minute intervals north and south along the Strip between the southernmost point, Vacation Village, and the northernmost point, the Downtown Transportation Center. From midnight to 5 a.m., the bus takes the same route but at 15-minute intervals. The Strip Express (Route 302) runs this same route daily at 15-minute intervals from southbound 6 p.m. to 1 a.m., northbound 5 p.m.-midnight.

The CAT bus (Route 303) provides hourly service from 5:30 a.m. to 10:30 a.m. and on the half hour from 10:30 a. m. to 6:30 p.m., from Vacation Village south to Belz Factory Outlet World and Factory Stores of America.

Local residential bus service to several areas, including Henderson and Boulder City, is also available. Call for more information.

Downtown Trolley *(702) 229-6024. Fares: adults, 50¢; ages 62 and over, ages 17 and under and disabled, 25¢.* Shuttle buses designed to look like trolleys depart the Downtown Transportation Center daily every 20 minutes from 7 a.m. to 11 p.m. The route traveled is along Ogden Ave.

(eastbound) to the Charleston Plaza Shopping Center and Fremont St. (westbound). The entire route takes 30 minutes to travel. (Do not confuse this trolley with the Strip trolley.) See the *Downtown Las Vegas* map.

Strip Trolley *(702) 382-1404. Fare: $1.40.* Like the downtown trolley, the Strip trolley also uses shuttle buses designed to look like trolleys. The trolleys operate daily 9:30 a.m. to 2 a.m. along Las Vegas Blvd. South from the Luxor on the south end to the Stratosphere Tower on the north end. An additional loop includes the Las Vegas Hilton and a portion of Paradise Rd. The trolleys pass by each stop about every 15 minutes. (Do not confuse this trolley with the downtown trolley.) See the *Las Vegas Strip* map.

Taxi *$2.20 base fare plus $1.50 per mile; 35¢ per minute for standing still. Pickups at McCarran International Airport pay $1.20 tax per load.* For visitors who come to Las Vegas to enjoy gaming and entertainment, a trouble-free and economical way of getting around is by cab. Taxis are plentiful, particularly at the entrances of the major resort hotels, and using them helps avoid the nuisance of having to find a parking space in a crowded lot. In addition, if two or three people share one taxi, it compares favorably to the cost of the bus, and there is usually no waiting. A typical trip half the length of the Strip will cost between $10 and $17; from the airport to the middle of the Strip, $10 to $12; and from the airport to downtown, $16 to $24.

Visitors who are staying at a hotel or motel not frequented by cabs or who wish to arrange for a taxi at a particular time may phone any of the following companies for service in Las Vegas. Upon request, ABC Union, Ace, NLV and Western provide vans with wheelchair lifts at regular taxi rates.

ABC Union	(702) 736-8444
Ace	(702) 736-8383
Checker/Star/Yellow	
	(702) 873-2227
Desert	(702) 386-9102
Henderson	(702) 384-2322
Nellis	(702) 252-0201
NLV	(702) 643-1041
Western	(702) 382-7100
Whittlesea Blue	(702) 384-6111

Hospitals

Desert Springs Hospital
2075 E. Flamingo Rd.
Las Vegas 89119
(702) 733-8800

Lake Mead Hospital Medical Center
1409 E. Lake Mead Blvd.
North Las Vegas 89030
(702) 649-7711

St. Rose Dominican Hospital
102 E. Lake Mead Dr.
Henderson 89015
(702) 564-2622

Sunrise Hospital and Medical Center
Sunrise Childrens Hospital
3186 S. Maryland Pkwy.
Las Vegas 89109
(702) 731-8000

University Medical Center
1800 W. Charleston Blvd.
Las Vegas 89102
(702) 383-2000

Valley Hospital Medical Center
620 Shadow Ln.
Las Vegas 89106
(702) 388-4000

AAA/California State Automobile Association

Henderson District Office
601 Whitney Ranch Dr., Ste. A
Henderson 89014
(702) 458-2323
Office hours: Mon.-Fri. 8:30 a.m.-5:30 p.m.

Las Vegas District Office
3312 W. Charleston Blvd.
Las Vegas 89102
(702) 870-9171
Office hours: Mon.-Fri. 8:30 a.m.-5:30 p.m.

Summerlin
8440 W. Lake Mead Blvd., Ste. 203
Las Vegas 89128
(702) 360-3151
Office hours: Mon.-Fri. 8:30-5:30 p.m.

Visitor Services

Boulder City Chamber of Commerce
1305 Arizona St.
Boulder City 89005
(702) 293-2034
Office hours: Mon.-Fri. 9 a.m.-5 p.m.

Las Vegas Convention and Visitors Authority
3150 Paradise Rd.
Las Vegas 89109
(702) 892-7575, 892-0711
Office hours: Mon.-Fri. 8 a.m.-6 p.m., Sat.-Sun. 8 a.m.-5 p.m.

Nevada Welcome Center
100 Nevada Hwy.
Boulder City 89005
No phone
Office hours: Daily 8:30 a.m.-4:30 p.m.

CIRCUS CIRCUS HOTEL & CASINO *2880 Las Vegas Blvd. S., 89109. (702) 734-0410.* **The Adventuredome** *Recorded information (702) 794-3939. Open daily 10 a.m.; closing times vary with season. $15.95 for 48"and taller; $11.95 for 33"-48"; individual ride ticket prices vary. Military and Nev. residents, $2 off adult unlimited-ride pass.* The Adventuredome is a climate-controlled amusement park spanning five acres. Featured rides include the nation's only indoor double-loop, double-corkscrew roller coaster; a water flume ride with a 60-foot free fall; Hot Shots Laser Tag, a high-tech version of the old game of tag; and a number of tamer attractions suitable for younger children. Themed gift shops, a restaurant and snack bar are also on premises.

The Midway *Under the big top. Open daily 11 a.m.-11 p.m. Performances every ½ hour. Free.* Circus acts include acrobatic antics on both the high and low wire, juggling, trapeze artists and unicycle balancing acts.

DOLPHIN AND SECRET GARDEN HABITATS—*See Mirage.*

EXCALIBUR HOTEL & CASINO *3850 Las Vegas Blvd. S., 89109. (702) 597-7777; (800) 937-7777. Dragon battle staged nightly on the hour, dusk-midnight; motion theater open daily 10 a.m.-11:30 p.m., $3 per person.* This huge, castle-shaped hotel is themed throughout after the medieval days of King Arthur. Among the attractions are two motion simulator theaters, medieval-themed midway games, strolling entertainers and the Court Jester's Stage, where performances take place throughout the day. Outside at the hotel's moat-style entrance, a fire-breathing dragon battles Merlin the magician nightly.

FACTORY STORES OF AMERICA *9155 Las Vegas Blvd. S., 89123. (702) 897-9090. Open daily; Mon.-Sat. 10 a.m.-8 p.m., Sun. to 6 p.m.* More than 50 factory outlet stores are featured at this open-air shopping center, including a sports bar with slot machines.

FASHION SHOW MALL *Next to Treasure Island, at corner of Las Vegas Blvd. S. and Spring Mountain Rd.; 3200 Las Vegas Blvd. S., 89109. (702) 369-8382. Open daily; Mon.-Fri. 10 a.m.-9 p.m., Sat. 10 a.m.-7 p.m., Sun. noon-6 p.m.* The enclosed, two-level mall houses five department stores and

Dive! restaurant is a prominent feature at the Fashion Show Mall.

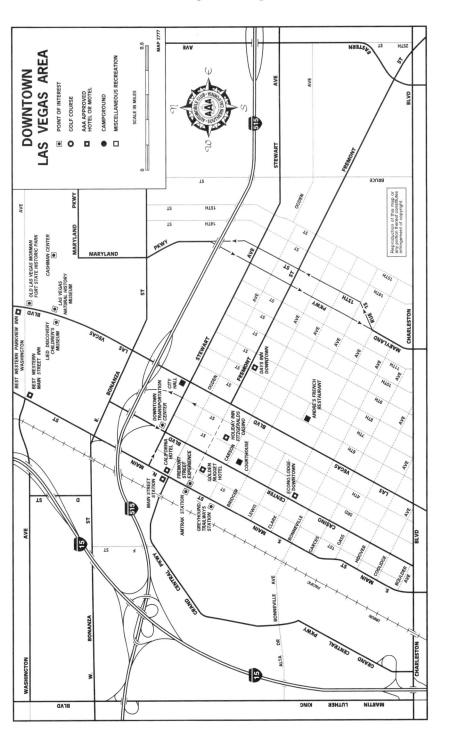

The Imperial Palace Auto Collection features changing exhibits of classic, antique and special-interest autos, trucks and motorcycles.

over 145 specialty shops and eateries, including the popular Dive! restaurant. Lighted underground parking accommodates more than 1500 cars.

GAMEWORKS *In Showcase Mall, 3785 Las Vegas Blvd. S.; 89108. (702) 432-4263. Open daily 10 a.m.- 2 a.m., Fri.-Sat. to 4 a.m. Game prices vary.* This two-level, virtual-reality arcade, created by Steven Spielberg, Sega Enterprises and Universal Studios, touts almost 300 video games of every description. Among the many attractions players can try their luck on are ski slopes, battlefields and raceways. The centerpiece is "Surge Rock," a 75-foot-tall rock-climbing structure. The facility also maintains a full-service bar and food services.

GUINNESS WORLD OF RECORDS MUSEUM AND GIFT SHOP *2780 Las Vegas Blvd. S., 89109. (702) 792-3766. Open daily at 9 a.m.; Labor Day to Memorial Day to 6 p.m., rest of year to 8 p.m. Adults, $4.95; ages 62 and over, students and military, $3.95; ages 5-11, $2.95.* Rare videos and artifacts commemorate the world's fastest, greatest, rarest and richest feats from the worlds of entertainment, art, sports and science. Literally thousands of records can be accessed from the

"Guinness World of Records" and "World of Sports" data banks. Displays offer visitors the chance to match their height with the world's tallest man and shortest woman, and their weight with that of the world's heaviest man. The "world" of Las Vegas is featured in a display highlighting the city's history, its casinos and entertainers.

HOLY COW CASINO, CAFE AND BREWERY *2423 Las Vegas Blvd. S., 89104. (702) 732-2697. Open 24 hours. Free tours 4 times daily; call for schedule. Parking lot adjacent.* Opened in 1992 as Las Vegas' original microbrewery, Holy Cow uses traditional brewing methods and features several award-winning brews. Cow enthusiasts will appreciate the cow accents throughout the interior and the "cowlectibles" sold in the gift shop. The restaurant serves a variety of American-style fare.

IMPERIAL PALACE AUTO COLLECTION *Imperial Palace Hotel, 3535 Las Vegas Blvd. S., 89109. (702) 794-3174. Open daily 9:30 a.m.-11:30 p.m. Adults, $6.95; ages 65 and over and 4-12, $3; under 3, free.* This auto museum, located on the fifth level of the hotel's parking structure, features more than 200 antique, classic and special-interest autos, antique trucks, motorcycles, and cars once owned by gangsters and world-famous celebrities. It also houses the world's largest collection of Model J Duesenbergs. The collection contains more than 800 vehicles, which are rotated on a bimonthly basis.

LAS VEGAS CONVENTION CENTER *3150 Paradise Rd., 89109. (702) 892-0711.* With 1.6 million square feet of meeting and exhibit space, the convention center is one of the largest single-level facilities in the world. The Las Vegas Convention Center offers more than 760,000 square feet of exhibit space and 97 meeting rooms totaling more 150,000 square feet, and an on-site restaurant. The facility can host small groups of people as well as conventions in excess of 200,000 people.

LAS VEGAS HILTON *From I-15, exit Flamingo Rd. E., then north on the Strip; 3555 Las Vegas Bl. S., 89109.*

Star Trek: The Experience *Open 11 a.m.-11 p.m. (702) 697-8751.*

Deep Space Nine the Promenade *Free.* At this dining and shopping experience, visitors mingle among Klingons, Ferengi and other Starfleet officers. Shopping may be accomplished at Zek's Grand Emporium, which houses the largest collection of officially licensed Star Trek merchandise. Dine in the 24th Century at Quark's Bar, where the menu includes such items as Romulan Ale (German pilsner), Glop on a Stick (corn dog) and The Wrap of Khan (chicken fajita wrap).

The Voyage Through Space *$14.95; minimum height 42".* This 22-minute excursion to the 24th century starts on the bridge of the USS *Enterprise.* After boarding a shuttlecraft, a four-minute simulated space battle ensues with the victors exiting to the Deep Space Nine

Promenade. Included in the Voyage Through Space is admission to The History of the Future, a self-guided exhibit of more than 200 Star Trek costumes and props from movies and television.

LAS VEGAS MINI GRAND PRIX *1401 N. Rainbow Blvd., 89108. (702) 259-7000. Open daily at 10 a.m.; Sun.-Thu. to 11 p.m.; Fri. and Sat. to midnight. Closed Dec. 25. $4 per ticket or $17.50 for 5.* This motor amusement center features racetracks where children and adults alike can test their driving skills. Vehicles range from "Kiddie Karts" and go-karts to grand prix cars and "super stock cars." Snack bar on site.

LAS VEGAS MOTOR SPEEDWAY *7000 Las Vegas Blvd. N., 89115. (702) 644-4444. Call for ticket prices and program information.* This racing complex hosts a wide range of events throughout the year, most prominently the Las Vegas 400 NASCAR race each March on the 1.5-mile oval. Several smaller tracks accommodate everything from drag racing to road course racing events.

University of Motor Sports *Various locations inside speedway. (702) 644-6433. Call for hours and price information.* Would-be race drivers can choose from among 15 different schools to learn racing techniques in a wide variety of vehicles. Options range from go-karts and BMX bicycles all the way up to dragsters and Winston Cup stock cars.

LAS VEGAS NATURAL HISTORY MUSEUM *900 Las Vegas Blvd. N., 89101. (702) 384-3466. Open daily 9 a.m.-4 p.m. Adults, $5; ages 55 and over, students and military, $4; ages 4-12, $2.50; ages 3 and under, free.* The museum features an animated dinosaurs exhibit, including a 35-foot tyran-

The Las Vegas Natural History Museum has one of the most complete exhibits of animated dinosaur replicas in the Southwest.

nosaurus rex; an international wildlife room with mounted animals including a giraffe; a 3000-gallon tank filled with live sharks; a display of plants and wildlife native to Southern Nevada and the Southwest desert; and a children's room that features hands-on exhibits. There is also a gift shop on premises.

THE LIBERACE MUSEUM *2 miles east of the Strip at 1775 E. Tropicana Ave., 89119. (702) 798-5595. Open daily to 5 p.m.; Mon.-Sat. from 10 a.m., Sun. from 1 p.m. Adults, $6.95; ages 13-18, 60 and over and students, $4.95; ages 12 and under, free. Children must be accompanied by an adult.* The museum's collection of memorabilia, antiques and classic cars includes Liberace's million-dollar wardrobe and extensive fur collection, his gold and diamond stage jewelry (including a diamond and platinum candelabra ring), and a Baldwin grand piano inlaid with thousands of etched mirror tiles. Of particular interest are a desk once owned by Czar Nicholas II, a piano that Chopin once played, and a crucifix presented to Liberace by Pope Pius XII. The museum also houses a library displaying his miniature piano collection, a photographic history of his life, and a re-creation of his former office and bedroom. Proceeds from the museum go to the nonprofit Liberace Foundation for the Performing and Creative Arts.

LIED DISCOVERY CHILDREN'S MUSEUM *833 Las Vegas Blvd. N., 89101. (702) 382-3445. Open Tue.-Sun. 10 a.m.-5 p.m. Closed Mon., except most school holidays. Adults, $5; military, ages 55 and over and 2-17, $4; under 2 and members, free.* More than 100 hands-on exhibits are featured in this large museum. Play areas include "Places and Spaces," "What Can I Be?" and "Everyday Living," as well as the Toddler Tower, the Bubble Pavilion and the Science Tower.

Lied Discovery Children's Museum features a number of intriguing exhibits for the younger set.

Eighteen rare and antique pianos are on display in the Piano Gallery at the Liberace Museum.

LUXOR LAS VEGAS *3900 Las Vegas Blvd. S., 89119. Recorded information (702) 262-4555.*

Luxor Entertainment Complex *Shows screen daily 10 a.m.-11 p.m., various shows start about every hour; call for specific show times. Show admissions $4-8.95 per person.* The Luxor transports guests back in time to a replica of the Tomb of Tutankhamun or to a yet-undeveloped manned space station "L 5," as it would be seen by a child. "In Search of the Obelisk" is a motion simulator ride that explores a fictional underground civilization. The Imax theater offers two- and three-dimensional movies.

MAGIC & MOVIE HALL OF FAME *3555 Las Vegas Blvd. S., 89109. (702) 737-1343; 737-5363. Open Tue.-Sat. 10 a.m.-6 p.m.; call for comedy-magic show times. $9.95 per person.* This museum features a multimillion dollar exhibit of magic, movie and ventriloquist memorabilia. Half-hour-long comedy-magic shows are included with the price of admission.

MANDALAY BAY RESORT & CASINO *3950 Las Vegas Blvd. S., 89119. (877) 632-7000; (702) 632-7777; FAX (702) 632-7190.*

House of Blues *As of press time, hours of operation had not been determined.* This live music venue includes a restaurant featuring Southern-inspired cuisine and a traditional Sunday gospel brunch.

Sand and Surf Beach *Call for hours of operation and admission prices.* Visitors to this 11-acre beach and wave pool may catch 3- to 5-foot swells or simply bask in the Las Vegas sun.

MEADOWS MALL *US 95 at Valley View; 4300 Meadows Ln., 89107. (702) 878-4849. Open daily at 10 a.m.; Mon.-Fri. to 9 p.m., Sat. to 7 p.m., Sun. to 6 p.m.; extended hours during Dec. holiday season. Carousel ride 50¢.* This enclosed mall features a 1920s-style, hand-painted carousel in its center court, and more than 140 national and regional retailers and restaurants.

MGM GRAND HOTEL CASINO & THEME PARK *3799 Las Vegas Blvd. S., 89109. (702) 891-7979.*

MGM Grand Adventures Theme Park *Open daily 10 a.m.-10 p.m. Free admission. Rides: ages 11 and older, $12; ages 2-10 (over 42"), $10.* The 18-acre complex has several major attractions, including a roller coaster, water rides, bumper cars and the world's largest sky coaster. There are also celebrity look-alikes, strolling performers, musical shows, eight themed areas, restaurants and shops.

MIRAGE *3400 Las Vegas Blvd. S., 89109. (702) 791-7111.*

Dolphin and Secrete Garden Habitats *Dolphin Habitat open daily; Mon.-Fri. 11 a.m.-5:30 p.m., Sat., Sun. and holidays 10 a.m.-5:30 p.m. Adults $10, on Wed. $5; ages 9 and under accompanied by an adult, free. White Tiger Habitat open 24 hours; free.* A close look at seven Atlantic bottle-nose dolphins is the main draw of the Dolphin Habitat, which offers continuous 15-minute tours focused primarily on the facility's underwater viewing room. The Secret Garden features eight zoological environments with animals from the Siegfried & Roy stage show. One of these habitats features the famous Royal White Tigers of the Siegfried & Roy stage show and is located on the hotel's southwestern side, just off the casino. Located behind a floor-to-ceiling wall of glass, these beautiful animals can be observed while they sleep, eat and play.

The Volcano *Shows daily dusk-midnight. Free.* Located at the hotel's front entrance, the volcano's fiery, smoke-belching explosions occur every few minutes and never fail to momentarily stop traffic on the famous Strip.

NELLIS AIR FORCE BASE

Main gate at Las Vegas Blvd. and Craig Rd. (702) 652-1110. Nellis, a weapons testing and tactical fighter training center, is also the home of the "Thunderbirds," the Air Force's precision flying team. The Thunderbirds are often away performing at air shows throughout the country, but they do perform at the Nellis AFB Open House, which is held every two years; call for schedule.

Thunderbird Museum *Located on the base (directions given at main gate). (702) 652-4018. Tours Tue. and Thu. at 2 p.m. Closed last 2 weeks of Dec.* The museum tour is open to the public and features a short program, film and close-up look at an F-16 static display.

NEVADA STATE MUSEUM AND HISTORICAL SOCIETY

Located in Lorenzi Park; 700 Twin Lakes Dr., 89107. (702) 486-5205. Open daily 9 a.m.-5 p.m. Closed Jan. 1, Thanksgiving and Dec. 25. Adults, $2; ages 17 and under, free. This lakeside museum has three main galleries, two of which focus on natural history and one that focuses on the history of the Southern Nevada region. A research library is also located here. American Indian jewelry, and books and videos about Nevada's history can be purchased in the museum store.

NEW YORK NEW YORK HOTEL & CASINO

3790 Las Vegas Blvd. S., 89109. (702) 740-6969. Manhattan Express roller coaster open daily 10 a.m.-10:30 p.m., Fri.-Sat. to 11 p.m. $4. Modeled through-

New York New York Hotel & Casino, which opened in 1997, is one example of the new wave of theme resorts to open along the Strip in recent years.

out after its namesake, New York New York is conspicuous with its 12 Manhattan-style hotel towers, and scale models of the Statue of Liberty and Brooklyn Bridge. Among the main attractions inside is the Coney Island Emporium, an arcade combining an early 1900s atmosphere and old-fashion midway games with the latest high-tech gadgetry. Next to the emporium is the 203-foot-tall Manhattan Express roller coaster. The hotel also features eateries that are themed after Greenwich Village and Little Italy.

OLD LAS VEGAS MORMON FORT STATE HISTORIC PARK

908 Las Vegas Blvd. N.; State Mail Room, Las Vegas 89158. (702) 486-3511. Call for hours. Donations accepted. The fort, built by Mormon settlers in 1855, is the oldest European-American building in the state of Nevada. It provided shelter for gold-seekers, emigrants and other travelers along the Spanish Trail/Mormon Road. At the turn of the 19th century, the fort was owned by the San Pedro, Los Angeles and Salt Lake Railroad (now part of Union Pacific); it also served as a resort, dairy and farm for the burgeoning new town of Las Vegas. Currently, sections of the Old Fort and adjacent ranch buildings are being restored. Historic photographs, interpretive panels and antiques from the mid-1800s are on display at the site.

PARIS-LAS VEGAS *3645 Las Vegas Blvd. S., 89109. (702) 739-4111.*

Eiffel Tower *As of press time, the hours of operation had not yet been determined.* The Eiffel Tower, originally constructed in France for the 1889 World's Fair, has been reconstructed to ½ scale on the Las Vegas Strip. A restaurant inside

Lush tropical foliage, lifelike animals and waterfalls can be found in Sam's Town indoor park.

Visible for miles, the Stratosphere Tower defines the northern end of the famous Strip.

Scandia Family Fun Center features all kinds of family fun,
including three 18-hole miniature golf courses,
Indy-style racers, bumper boats and a large video game arcade.

the superstructure is 100 feet above the Strip. Guests may also take a glass elevator to an observation deck on the 50th story.

SAHARA PAVILIONS *Northeast and southeast corners of Sahara Ave. and Decatur Blvd.; 4760 W. Sahara, 89102. (702) 258-4330. Hours vary by store, some open 24 hours.* This 487,000-square-foot mall has a total of 95 stores, restaurants and services.

SAM'S TOWN HOTEL *5111 Boulder Hwy., 89122. (702) 456-7777.*

Sam's Town Mystic Falls Park Laser, Light and Water Show *Laser show daily at 2, 6, 8 and 10 p.m. Free.* A nine-story atrium encloses this 25,000-square-foot indoor park, which houses lifelike animals, lush tropical foliage, waterfalls and meandering footpaths. Restaurants with patio seating, shops and the hotel itself surround the park. The western-themed laser, light and water show is presented four times daily and features music, laser animation and synchronized show fountains.

SCANDIA FAMILY FUN CENTER *On the west side of I-15, south of Sahara Ave.; 2900 Sirius Ave., 89102. (702) 364-0070. Open 24 hours. Unlimited all-day wristband, $15.95; Supersaver all-attraction pass, $10.95; individual ride admissions available.* This amusement center features miniature Indy-type race cars, three elaborate 18-hole miniature golf courses, bumper boats, baseball batting cages and a large video game arcade. Snack bar on site.

SOUTHERN NEVADA ZOOLOGICAL-BOTANICAL PARK *3 miles northwest of downtown; 1775 N. Rancho Dr., 89106. (702) 648-5955; 647-4685. Open daily 9 a.m.-4:30 p.m. Closed Jan. 1, Thanksgiving and Dec. 25. Adults, $5.95; ages 2-12 and 60 and over, $3.95.*
Children will enjoy this small zoological-botanical park, which exhibits a collection of mostly small animals and exotic birds. Featured are the last family of Barbary apes in the U.S., animals ranging from alligators to tigers, and all the venomous reptiles found in Southern Nevada. Birds on display range from talking parrots and ravens to golden eagles and ostriches. A snack bar and gift shop are located on the grounds. Off-road tours of the surrounding desert area that includes the perimeter of "Area-51" are also available.

STRATOSPHERE TOWER *2000 Las Vegas Blvd. S., 89104. (702) 380-7777, (800) 998-6937. Sun.-Thu. 10 a.m.-1 a.m., Fri.-Sat. 10 a.m.-2 a.m. Call for prices and further information.*
The focus of the Stratosphere Hotel and Casino is the tower rising 1149 feet above the Strip. The tallest, free-standing observation tower in the United States, it is 156 feet taller than the Eiffel Tower in Paris. An eye-catching sight with its futuristic, Space Needle-like appearance and soaring height, it features two observation platforms, a revolving restaurant with 360-degree views, cocktail lounge, meeting rooms, two thrill rides (including the world's highest roller coaster and a free-fall ride), and a retail/entertainment complex.

TREASURE ISLAND *3300 Las Vegas Blvd. S., 89109. (702) 894-7111.*

Buccaneer Bay *Shows daily at 4, 5:30, 7, 8:30, 10 and 11:30 p.m.; no performances during inclement weather or high winds. Arrive early for best viewing; standing room only. Free.* Located at the hotel's main entrance on the Strip, Buccaneer Bay treats passersby to a highly entertaining sea battle between an 80-foot-long pirate ship and a British frigate. The show features live actors, numerous fiery explosions and lots of witty, swashbuckling dialogue.

UNIVERSITY OF NEVADA, LAS VEGAS *4505 S. Maryland Pkwy., 89154. (702) 895-3011; campus tours (702) 895-3443.* More than 20,000 students attend classes on the 335-acre campus. The school's curricula include courses in art and architecture, engineering, law, mathematics, science and a lengthy list of other subjects. The university's first building, Maude Frazier Hall, opened its doors in 1957. After a brief stint as Nevada Southern University, the campus was given autonomy and equality in 1968 with the University of Nevada, Reno, and renamed in 1969. For campus tours, call or drop by the admissions office, Maude Frazier Hall, Room 114. A brochure for the self-guided arboretum tour of the campus is available from the UNLV News and Public Information Office, the Museum of Natural History and the grounds department.

Artemus W. Ham Concert Hall, Judy Bayley Theatre and **Alta Ham Black Box Theatre** *Adjacent to Maryland Pkwy.; north end of Academic Mall. Schedule and ticket information (702) 895-3801. Tickets range in price from free to $75.* These three facilities form the campus' Performing Arts Center. The center regularly presents major international performing artists in classical and popular music, dance, theater and opera. It is also home to the Nevada Symphony Orchestra, Nevada Opera-Theatre and the Community Concert Association, whose seasons run from September through May and include professional performances in ballet, symphonic and chamber music, and opera.

Donna Beam Fine Art Gallery *In the Alta Ham Fine Arts Bldg., Room 145-A. (702) 895-3893. Open Mon.-Fri. 9 a.m.-5 p.m. Closed Sat., Sun. and major holidays. Free.* The gallery hosts changing exhibitions by students, faculty and invited artists.

Flashlight *Between the Artemus W. Ham Concert Hall and the Judy Bayley Theatre; north end of Academic Mall.* This striking 38-foot-high, 74,000-pound steel sculpture was fashioned by acclaimed artists Claes Oldenberg and Coosje van Bruggen.

Marjorie Barrick Museum of Natural History *On campus; east of Swenson St. at end of Harmon Ave. Metered parking adjacent to museum. (702) 895-3381. Open Mon.-Fri. 9 a.m.-4:45 p.m., Sat. 10 a.m.-2 p.m. Closed Sun. and holidays. Free.* The museum encompasses permanent exhibits on the archaeology, geology and biology of the desert Southwest, an outdoor botanical garden and taxidermy displays of indigenous animals.

Sam Boyd Stadium *Off campus; via US 93/95 (use Russell Rd. exit) in Silver Bowl Regional Park. Ticket information (702) 895-3900.* The stadium is home to the university's NCAA football team, the Rebels, from September through November. It also hosts motocross competitions and concerts in the summer.

Thomas and Mack Center *Off Tropicana Ave. at Swenson St. Events*

Wet 'n Wild offers relief from the hot Las Vegas sun.

Surrounded by a stark desert landscape, Floyd Lamb State Park emerges as an oasis of tree-shaded groves and gentle beauty. The park's four small lakes are stocked with rainbow trout in winter and catfish in summer.

schedule and ticket information (702) 895-3900. This 18,500-seat indoor arena hosts sporting events, concerts and shows. From November through February it is the home court for the school's NCAA Runnin' Rebels Big West basketball team.

VEGAS POINTE PLAZA *9155 Las Vegas Blvd. S., 89123. (702) 897-9090. Open daily at 10 a.m.; Mon.-Sat. to 8 p.m., Sun. to 6 p.m.* More than 35 factory outlet stores are featured at this open-air shopping center, including a sports bar with slot machines.

THE VOLCANO—*See Mirage.*

WET 'N WILD *2601 Las Vegas Blvd. S., 89109. (702) 734-0088. Open May through Sep., daily at 10 a.m.; closing time varies. Adults, $24.95; ages 55 and over, $13; ages 3-9, $18.95.* This 26-acre, family-oriented water park features "Willy Willy," a hydra-hurricane ride; "Banzai Banzai," a water roller coaster; and "Der Stuka," a 76-foot-high water slide. In addition, there are rapids, a 500,000-gallon wave pool, a surf lagoon and a children's pool. There are also areas for sunbathing and picnicking. (**See ad next page.**)

WORLD OF COCA-COLA LAS VEGAS *In Showcase Mall at 3785 Las Vegas Blvd. S.; 89109. (702) 270-5965, (800) 720-2653. Open daily 10 a.m.-midnight; Fri.-Sat. to 1 a.m. Admission for age 3 and over, $2; ages 2 and under, free.* A museum and bottling plant in one, the World of Coca-Cola immerses visitors in the history and lore surrounding the venerable soft drink. Coca-Cola art, vintage commercials, a life-size soda fountain and free samples are among the attractions. The building's centerpiece is a 100-foot-tall Coke bottle, in which visitors ride to the top to begin the Coca-Cola "experience."

North Las Vegas

See **A Quick Guide to Las Vegas** in this chapter under Las Vegas.

FLOYD LAMB STATE PARK *15 miles northwest of Las Vegas off US 95; east from 395 at Durango; 9200 Tule Springs Rd., Las Vegas 89131. (702) 486-5413. Open daily 8 a.m.-dusk. Closed Jan. 1 and Dec. 25. Entrance fee: $5 per vehicle.* The park encompasses 2040 acres, including **Tule Springs Ranch**, four small lakes and the surrounding natural desert area. Fishing is permitted in all four lakes, and all are stocked with rainbow trout in winter and catfish in summer. Largemouth bass live in the lakes, but the catch is low. Swimming, wading and boating are not allowed. Picnic tables and grills are located throughout the park and are available on a first-come, first-

served basis. Self-guided hiking trails traverse tree-shaded groves and pass by the lakes.

The Tule Springs area has long been known as one of the best Pleistocene fossil sites in western North America. Remains found here have included giant sloths, bison, camels, horses and mammoths. Man's first presence in the area, however, only dates back 10,000 to 11,000 years. Today that presence is much more in evidence. The area that is now Floyd Lamb State Park was used as a watering stop by American Indians and local prospectors, and as a rest stop for horses on the Bullfrog Stage Line to Rhyolite. John Herbert Nay began farming the land in 1916, but sold the land in 1928. It remained vacant until 1941 when Jacob Goumond turned it into a working ranch.

When Nevada's divorce laws became the most liberal in the country by requiring only a six-week residency, Goumond saw a chance to make money with a "dude" ranch. Divorcees who came to live out their residency requirements occupied themselves with horseback riding, swimming, tennis, hayrides, barbecues, dances and a shooting range. But even as a dude ranch, Tule Springs remained a working farm. Livestock included a herd of cattle, dairy cows, horses, chickens, turkeys and pigs. Fruits and vegetables were grown year round and 100 acres were cultivated in alfalfa. Ranch denizens today include peacocks, ducks

and geese. Visitors may roam the grounds of the old Tule Springs Ranch. A group of 22 historic structures are currently used only by park staff; future plans call for rehabilitation of the site. The buildings are identified in a park brochure, available at the entrance station.

G U I D E D   T O U R S

The tours listed in this section generally last less than a day, though some of the trips to more distant places involve an overnight stay. Be sure to contact the companies in advance for complete information and reservations; many tours offer hotel pickup and discounted children's rates. Also, check refund policies to avoid losing your deposit in the event of a late cancellation. Scheduled tours are subject to cancellation if there is an insufficient number of passengers.

Tours listed are provided as a convenience for our readers; inclusion in this publication does not imply endorsement by the Automobile Club of Southern California.

Las Vegas

AIR VEGAS AIRLINES *Henderson Executive Airport; P.O. Box 11008, 89111. (702) 736-3599, (800) 255-7474; FAX (702) 361-8967.* Grand Canyon; charter flights to Bryce Canyon; Monument Valley air and land tours.

CACTUS JACK'S WILD WEST TOUR COMPANY *2217 Paradise Rd., Ste. A, 89104. (702) 731-5902;*

▼ *Grand Canyon Flights*

In 1987 the U.S. Congress passed a law prohibiting flights below the canyon rim, and directed the National Park Service (NPS) and the Federal Aviation Administration (FAA) to designate safe routes for flights over the national park area. The NPS then proposed to the FAA that flight-free zones be established over 45 percent of the Grand Canyon, that air-tour operators be restricted to flying in specific routes over the least-used parts of the park, and that pilots be required to stay above the canyon rim. The law took effect in September 1988. An environmental impact study on these overflights was conducted and submitted to Congress in 1994. The NPS and FAA are working together to develop a final use plan for the canyon that may restrict the number of flights and/or the noise level that the flights may generate. According to a government spokesperson, those flying over the canyon can still view much of the grandeur of the park. The main concerns are passenger safety and the noise level. Future guidelines are due to take affect in January of 2000.

Majestic Hoover Dam is a popular guided tour destination.

FAX *(702) 731-5902.* Grand Canyon, Lake Mead, Hoover Dam, and Laughlin air/land and land tours.

DESTINATION LAS VEGAS UNLIMITED *1050 E. Flamingo Rd., 89119. (702) 733-6060; FAX (702) 733-6611.* Grand Canyon, Hoover Dam, Lake Mead and Laughlin air and land tours.

EAGLE CANYON AIRLINES *275 E. Tropicana, Ste. 220, 89109.*

(702) 740-8300, (800) 446-4584; FAX (702) 736-3333. Grand Canyon air and land tours. **(See ad below.)**

GRAY LINE TOURS *4020 E. Lone Mountain Rd., 89031. (702) 644-2233; FAX (702) 644-2477.* Grand Canyon, Colorado River, Hoover Dam/Lake Mead, Valley of Fire/Lost City Museum of Archeology, Red Rock Canyon/Mount Charleston, Las Vegas, Laughlin land tours and air/land packages.

GUARANTEED TOURS *3734 Las Vegas Blvd., Ste. 4, 89109. (800) 777-4697; FAX (702) 795-8735.* Laughlin, Hoover Dam, Grand Canyon, Zion, Death Valley, Lake Mead and Red Rock land and air tours. **(See ad page 50.)**

KEY TOURS *3305 W. Spring Mountain Rd., Ste. 16, 89102. (702) 362-9355.* Hoover Dam, Laughlin and Primm land tours. Departures from the Four Queens, Silver City, Flamingo Hilton, Circus Circus, Harrah's, Excalibur and Tropicana hotels.

SCENIC TOURS *2705 Airport Dr., North Las Vegas, 89030. (702) 638-3300; FAX (702) 798-7066.* Grand Canyon, Colorado River, Hoover Dam/Lake Mead, Las Vegas, Laughlin; Primm and Zion National Park land tours.

SHOWTIME TOURS OF LAS VEGAS *4699 S. Industrial Rd., Ste. 14, 89103. (702) 895-8822; FAX*

*Flights over Grand Canyon National Park are popular
with Las Vegas visitors.*

(702) 895-9366. Grand Canyon, Hoover Dam, Laughlin air and air/land tours.

SIGHTSEEING TOURS UNLIMITED (STU) *4740 S. Valley View, 89103. (702) 471-7155.* Grand Canyon, Hoover Dam, Lake Mead, Las Vegas, Laughlin, river rafting, off-road Hummer tours, air and land tours.

SUNDANCE HELICOPTERS, INC. *5616 Haven St., 89119.*

(702) 736-0606, (800) 653-1881; FAX (702) 736-4107. Grand Canyon, Hoover Dam/Lake Mead and Las Vegas helicopter tours.

North Las Vegas

SCENIC AIRLINES *2705 Airport Dr., 89030. (702) 638-3300, (800) 634-6801 (outside Nev.); FAX (702) 638-3275.* Grand Canyon, Monument Valley, Bryce Canyon National Park, Phoenix, Lake Powell air/land tours.

SHOWROOM ENTERTAINMENT

Headline entertainment is second only to gambling in the number of visitors it attracts to Las Vegas. The big showrooms feature either a well-known singer or comedian backed by an opening act, or a glitzy production number with elaborate sets and costumes. Facilities listed here seat 500 or more. Showroom listing does not imply AAA endorsement for the lodging establishment. For the most current information, refer to the Auto Club's Las Vegas Shows schedule, available to AAA members at all district offices.

Tickets for production shows can be purchased by phoning or visiting the hotel's showroom box office or by contacting a local ticket agency. There are a number of ticket agencies in Las Vegas that specialize in booking entertainment. Refer to the telephone directory yellow pages under "Ticket Sales/Events" or "Tourist Information."

Many showrooms offer advance ticket sales and reserved seating. Be sure to ask at the time of purchase if the seats are reserved. If you have assigned seats, you should arrive approximately 20 minutes prior to show time. If seats are not assigned, then it is advisable to arrive at least an hour prior to curtain. As for dinner shows, remember that the time given is performance time. You should generally arrive two hours before show time for a dinner performance.

The prices listed for each show may not include the 7 percent sales tax, 10 percent entertainment tax or any gratuities. In addition to these extra charges, the prices will often be raised for some especially popular entertainers, as well as for opening and closing nights.

Large production shows often run indefinitely, many of them for several years. As of press time, shows scheduled to run indefinitely appear in the listings, but **any show is subject to change without notice. You are advised to verify shows, times and prices in advance.**

Although the early and late shows are basically the same in terms of content, children are not admitted to the late shows. The hour alone prevents most children from enjoying themselves, and entertainers like to feel freer to use language and discuss subjects that might not be appropriate for a general audience. For this reason, not only children but sensitive adults should attend the early shows. Production shows with nudity usually do not admit children; call the theater's box office in advance for any age restrictions that may apply.

Las Vegas

BALLY'S LAS VEGAS
3645 Las Vegas Blvd. S. (702) 739-4567.

Celebrity Room — Top-name entertainment. *Times and prices vary with entertainers.*

Jubilee Theatre — "Jubilee" (Indefinitely). *Sat.-Thu. 8 and 11 p.m.,*

Elaborate stage productions entertain thousands of visitors with dazzling sets and beautiful dancers.

except Sun. and Mon. 8 p.m. only. Dark Fri. $49.50-66 per person. Minimum age 18.

CAESARS PALACE
3570 Las Vegas Blvd. S. (702) 731-7333.

Circus Maximus — Top-name entertainment. *Times and prices vary with entertainers. Minimum age 6. Tickets can be purchased 30 days in advance by phone.*

THE DESERT INN
3145 Las Vegas Blvd. S. (702) 733-4566.

Crystal Room — Top-name entertainment. *Times and prices vary with entertainers. Smoke-free theater.*

EXCALIBUR HOTEL & CASINO
3850 Las Vegas Blvd. S. (702) 597-7600, (800) 933-1334.

King Arthur's Arena — "King Arthur's Tournament" (Indefinitely). *Nightly dinner shows at 6 and 8:30 p.m. $29.95 per person. Tickets can be purchased 6 days in advance by phone or at box office.*

FLAMINGO HILTON-LAS VEGAS
3555 Las Vegas Blvd. S. (702) 733-3333, (800) 221-7299.

Flamingo Showroom — "The Great Radio City Music Hall Spectacular, Starring the Rockettes" (Indefinitely). *Sat.-Thu. Dark Fri. Dinner show: 7:45 p.m., from $49.50 per person. Show only: 10:30 p.m., $42.50 per person.*

HARD ROCK HOTEL AND CASINO
4455 Paradise Rd. (702) 226-4650.

The Joint — Top-name entertainment. *Times and prices vary with entertainers. Tickets also sold at hotel box office and through Ticketmaster.*

HARRAH'S-LAS VEGAS
3475 Las Vegas Blvd. S. (702) 369-5222.

Commander's Theatre — "Spellbound —Starring Joaquin Ayala" (Indefinitely). *Mon.-Sat. 7:30 and 10 p.m. Dark Sun. $37.95 per person. Minimum age 5.*

IMPERIAL PALACE
3535 Las Vegas Blvd. S. (702) 794-3261.

Imperial Theatre — "Legends in Concert" (Indefinitely). *Mon.-Sat. 7:30 and 10:30 p.m. Dark Sun. $34.50 per person; ages 2-12, $19.50; younger than 2, free. Smoke-free theater.*

LAS VEGAS HILTON
3000 Paradise Rd. (702) 732-5755.

Hilton Showroom — Top-name entertainment. *Times and prices vary with entertainers.*

MGM GRAND HOTEL CASINO & THEME PARK
3799 Las Vegas Blvd. S. (702) 891-7777, (800) 929-1111.

Hollywood Theatre — Top-name entertainment. *Times and prices vary with entertainers.*

MGM Grand Garden Arena — Top-name entertainment/special events. *Times and prices vary with entertainers.*

Good battles evil in Excalibur's knightly dinner spectacular, "King Arthur's Tournament."

MGM Grand Theatre — "EFX! Starring Tommy Tune" (Indefinitely). *Tue.-Sat. 7:30 and 10:30 p.m. Dark Sun. and Mon. $51.50-72 per person.*

THE MIRAGE
3400 Las Vegas Blvd. S. (702) 791-7111, (702) 792-7777.

Siegfried and Roy Theatre — "Siegfried and Roy at the Mirage" (Indefinitely). *Fri.-Tue. 7:30 and 11 p.m. Dark Wed., Thu., Jun. and Nov. 24 to Dec. 29. $89.35 per person. Minimum age 5. Tickets can be purchased 7 days in advance.*

MONTE CARLO RESORT & CASINO
3770 Las Vegas Blvd. S. (702) 730-7000, (800) 311-8999.

Lance Burton Theatre — "Lance Burton, Master Magician" (Indefinitely). *Tue.-Sat. 7:30 and 10:30 p.m. Dark Sun. and Mon. $34.95-39.95 per person.*

NEW YORK NEW YORK HOTEL & CASINO
3790 Las Vegas Blvd. S. (702) 740-6815.

The Broadway Theatre — "The Lord of the Dance" (Indefinitely). *Tue., Wed. and Sat. 7:30 and 10:30 p.m.; Thu. and Fri. 9 p.m. Dark Mon. $50-60 per person.*

THE ORLEANS
4500 W. Tropicana Ave. (702) 365-7075.

Branson Theatre — Top-name entertainment. *Times and prices vary with entertainers.*

Cirque du Soleil is famous for its cutting-edge acrobatics, unusual music and old European theatrics.

RIO SUITE HOTEL & CASINO
3700 Flamingo Rd. (702) 252-7777.

Copacabana Showroom — "Danny Gans: The Man of Many Voices" (Indefinitely). *Wed.-Sun. 8 p.m. Dark Mon. and Tue. $60 per person.*

RIVIERA HOTEL
2901 Las Vegas Blvd. S. (702) 794-9433 (Mardi Gras Plaza); (702) 477-5274 (Versailles Theatre).

Mardi Gras Plaza — "An Evening at La Cage" (Indefinitely). *Wed.-Mon. 7:30 and 9:30 p.m., additional 11:15 p.m. show Wed. and Sat. Dark Tue. Show and buffet, $27.95 per person; show only, $21.95.*

Versailles Theatre — "Splash" (Indefinitely). *Nightly 7:30 and 10:30 p.m. $39.50-49.50 per person.*

Minimum age 18; call for information on 7:30 p.m. summer family show.

SAHARA HOTEL
2535 Las Vegas Blvd. S. (702) 737-2111.

Congo Room —Top-name entertainment. *Times and prices vary with entertainers. Smoke-free theater.*

STARDUST HOTEL
3000 Las Vegas Blvd. S. (702) 732-6325, (800) 824-6033.

Stardust Theatre — "Enter the Night" (Indefinitely). *Tue.-Thu. and Sat. 7:30 and 10:30 p.m., Sun. and Mon. 8 p.m. Dark Fri. $26.90 per person.*

STRATOSPHERE HOTEL & CASINO
2000 Las Vegas Blvd. S. (702) 380-7777, (800) 998-6937.

Broadway Showroom — "American Superstars" (Indefinitely). *Fri.-Wed. 7 and 10 p.m. Dark Thu. $22.95 for adults; ages 5-12 $16.95 per person.*

"Viva Las Vegas" (Indefinitely). *Mon.-Sat. 2 and 4 p.m. Dark Sun. $10 per person.*

TREASURE ISLAND
3300 Las Vegas Blvd. S. (702) 894-7722, (800) 392-1999.

Treasure Island Showroom — "Cirque du Soleil—Mystère" (Indefinitely). *Wed.-Sun. 7:30 and 10:30 p.m. Dark Mon. and Tue. $64.50 per person. Tickets can be purchased 7 days in advance by phone.*

TROPICANA RESORT AND CASINO
3801 Las Vegas Blvd. S. (702) 739-2411, (800) 468-9494.

Tiffany Theatre — "Folies Bergere" (Indefinitely). *Fri.-Wed. 8 and 10:30 p.m. Dark Thu. $49.75-59.75 per person. Minimum age 16.*

"Rick Thomas—Illusionist" *(Indefinitely). Daily 2 and 4 p.m. Dark Fri. $15.95-20.95 per person. Minimum age 5.*

ANNUAL EVENTS

Parades, rodeos, art fairs, fireworks displays and golf tournaments are just a few of the many annual community events that Las Vegas and environs have to offer. For detailed information about each event, please call the telephone numbers shown, or consult with the local chamber of commerce or visitor information bureau. In addition, casino tournaments take place throughout the year. In Las Vegas, spectator sports range from boxing to baseball, soccer to football and basketball to hockey.

Spectator sports are popular throughout the year in the Las Vegas area. The Las Vegas Stars baseball club (702-386-7200), affiliated with the San

Diego Padres of the National League, plays its home games at Cashman Field April through September. The Thomas & Mack Center is the home of two

*On your mark, get set, go! Runners take to the streets in the
Las Vegas International Marathon.*

teams: the International Hockey League's Las Vegas Thunder (702-798-7825), from October through April; and UNLV's NCAA Big West basketball team, the Runnin' Rebels (702-895-3900), who play November through February. Sam Boyd Stadium is the home venue for Rebels university football; the season runs September through November.

Auto racing is a fast-growing sport at the Las Vegas Motor Speedway, which hosts the Las Vegas 400 NASCAR race in March and many other events throughout the year. For more information, call (702) 644-4444. Other exciting sporting events throughout the year include WBA and WBC boxing matches at the Las Vegas Hilton, Caesars Palace and MGM Grand hotels; and ESPN Top Rank boxing matches at Bally's Casino Resort.

Casino tournaments in bridge, blackjack, slot play, craps, poker, gin rummy and bowling take place in many casinos. Anyone interested in these tournaments should contact the hotel or venue directly for dates and play information; room reservations should be made well in advance, as room space is often at a premium during a tournament.

February

LAS VEGAS INTERNATIONAL MARATHON *(702) 240-2722.* The full marathon has been run every year since 1967 and the half-marathon has been run since 1993; both finish in Las Vegas at Sunset Park. The half-marathon starts in Sloan, Nev., and the full marathon starts in Jean, Nev. Each event attracts more than 6000 participants from all 50 states and more than 35 countries.

March

FLYING COLORS KITE EXPO
Silver Bowl Sports Complex, Las Vegas, Nev. (702) 455-8206. This one-day

event offers free kite workshops, demonstrations and contests for all ages.

NATIVE AMERICAN ARTS FESTIVAL *Clark County Heritage Museum, Henderson, Nev. (702) 455-7955.* American Indian food and art, dancing, craft demonstrations and storytelling are featured during this three-day festival.

April

HENDERSON HERITAGE DAYS *Various locations, Henderson, Nev. (702) 565-8951.* This 10-day event celebrates Henderson's heritage with a beauty pageant, jazz, chili cookoff, car show, baseball tournament, street dances and parade.

May

LAS VEGAS SENIOR CLASSIC BY TRUEGREEN-CHEMLAWN *Tournament Players Club at The Canyons, Summerlin, Nev. (702) 242-3000.* This event is a three-day Senior PGA Tour golf tournament.

THE LAS VEGAS HELLDORADO DAYS RODEO *Thomas & Mack Center, Las Vegas, Nev. (702) 796-3557.* This four-day event commemorates Las Vegas' Western heritage with a PRCA rodeo and a $1 million bull-riding event.

CRAFT FAIR AND RIB BURN-OFF *Sunset Park, Las Vegas, Nev. (702) 455-8206.* Craft booths, barbecue, live music and children's activities round out the festivities during this two-day event.

June

KKLZ JUNEFEST *Silver Bowl Park, Las Vegas, Nev. (702) 739-9600.* Classic rock bands perform at the park on the first Saturday of the month.

September

LAS VEGAS MARIACHI FESTIVAL *Thomas & Mack Center Las Vegas, Nev. (800) 637-1006.* This day-long mariachi festival is one of the most prestigious of its kind in the U.S.

October

HENDERSON EXPO *Convention Center, Henderson, Nev. (702) 565-8951.* This three-day business expo features arts and crafts, a new car show, and a carnival.

LAS VEGAS BALLOON CLASSIC *Silver Bowl Park, Las Vegas, Nev. (702) 452-8066.* Hot air balloons compete for the Nevada "Silver State" Championship during this three-day event. Craft booths, food and entertainment are featured.

LAS VEGAS INVITATIONAL GOLF TOURNAMENT *Desert Inn Golf Club, Las Vegas Country Club and TPC at Summerlin. (702) 242-3000.* This PGA tour event lasts five days.

LAS VEGAS JAYCEES STATE FAIR *Cashman Field, Las Vegas, Nev. (702) 457-8832. Sometimes held in Sep.* Livestock exhibits, a carnival midway and crafts booths are featured at this six-day event.

RENAISSANCE FAIRE *Sunset Park, Las Vegas, Nev. (702) 455-8200.*

The National Finals Rodeo brings PRCA events to the Thomas & Mack Center in Las Vegas.

Historical reenactments, jousting, theatrical performances, food and strolling minstrels highlight this two-day event.

November

PAGENET-TOUR CHAMPION-SHIP *Desert Inn Golf Club, Las Vegas, Nev. (888) 254-4653.* The top 30 women's professional golfers on the LPGA Tour compete in this week-long event.

December

CHILDREN'S CHRISTMAS PARADE *Water St., Henderson, Nev. (702) 565-8951.* Held on a Saturday, this parade features floats, horses and a visit from Santa Claus.

NATIONAL FINALS RODEO *UNLV's Thomas & Mack Center, Las Vegas, Nev. (702) 895-3900.* This professional rodeo event takes place over 10 days and features saddle bronco, bareback and bull riding; calf roping; steer wrestling; and barrel racing.

NEW YEAR'S EVE CELEBRA-TIONS *Various locations. (702) 892-7575.*

USA NATIONAL TABLE TENNIS CHAMPIONSHIPS *Las Vegas Convention Center. (719) 578-4583.* Table tennis players compete over five days in divisions ranging from Men's and Women's Singles to Elementary Boys and Girls.

WINTER WONDERLAND *Sunset Park, Las Vegas, Nev. (702) 455-8200.* The winter season is celebrated with a day of reindeer games, ice-carving demonstrations, snow play (weather permitting) and live entertainment.

Outside Las Vegas

*From the grandeur of Hoover Dam to the pine forests of Mount Charleston, a world of opportunities beckons those who venture beyond the neon lights and go-go atmosphere of Las Vegas. Most of the surrounding region remains undeveloped, with a host of opportunities awaiting the adventurous traveler. To the southeast of Las Vegas is **Boulder City**, a tidy town that has maintained its down-home, historic atmosphere. The town serves as gateway to Hoover Dam and the many diversions of **Lake Mead National Recreation Area**. For breathtaking desert views, head west to **Red Rock National Conservation Area** or northeast to **Valley of Fire State Park**, both within an hour's drive of the Strip. Close as well is **Spring Mountains National Recreation Area**, home of Mount Charleston, the third highest peak in Nevada; it's less than an hour's drive to the northwest. At the California-Nevada border, the tiny town of **Primm** has emerged as a family entertainment center. Thanks to the "Desperado" roller-coaster and other thrill rides, this former drive-through hamlet has become a tourist destination in its own right.*

POINTS OF INTEREST

Attractions are listed alphabetically by city or area – **Boulder City, Lake Mead National Recreation Area, Overton, Primm, Red Rock Canyon National Conservation Area, Spring Mountains National Recreation Area** and **Valley of Fire State Park**. Listings in this chapter of attractions located on hotel properties do not necessarily imply AAA approval of the lodging facilities.

See **A Quick Guide to Las Vegas and Vicinity** in the *Las Vegas Valley* chapter for information on the areas included in this chapter.

Boulder City

BOULDER CITY HISTORIC DISTRICT *23 miles southeast of Las Vegas via US 93/95 on US 93/Nevada Hwy.* **Chamber of Commerce** *located at 1305 Arizona St., 89005. (702) 293-2034.* Boulder City was created to house the thousands of workers who built nearby Hoover Dam. It also takes a place in American history as this country's first fully developed, master-planned community. Listed on the National Register of Historic Places, Boulder City provides a glimpse into an earlier era, an oasis of Americana in the vast Southern Nevada desert.

Among Boulder City's many historic buildings, visitors will encounter numerous parks, generous landscaping, wide avenues lined with vintage street lamps, and charming, well-kept homes. Interestingly, this community of 15,130 is also the only city in Nevada where gaming has always been, and still is, illegal.

The construction of Boulder City began in 1931 and continued nonstop for nearly two years. While the rest of the country struggled during the Great Depression, this sparkling new community thrived—the population swelled to more than 8000 while the dam was being built. At that time Boulder City was the third largest city in Nevada.

Through the 1940s, Boulder City flourished as a regional government center and tourism point for the dam and Lake Mead. However, the community remained under the jurisdiction of the federal government, ensuring its proper development under the original plan. It took an act of Congress for Boulder City to become an incorporated municipality. The act passed and was signed on July 9, 1958, and Boulder City was incorporated on January 4, 1960.

A self-guided tour of the Boulder City Historic District is outlined in a brochure available at the local chamber of commerce. The historic district is divided into five major areas, including parks and public buildings, three residential sections and a commercial district. The city's best-known historic structure and focal point is the **Boulder Dam Hotel**, a pine-shingled, Dutch Colonial-style building on Arizona Street. Built in 1933 to accommodate a growing tourist industry, the 33-room hotel was Southern Nevada's finest inn,

boasting private baths and showers in each room—a rarity for the times—and an elegant lobby paneled in rare southern gumwood. The hotel hosted a steady stream of Hollywood celebrities, American politicians, European aristocrats and Far Eastern royalty. Currently, the Boulder Dam Hotel is the home of the Boulder City Chamber of Commerce, the Boulder City/Hoover Dam Museum, and the Boulder City Arts Council and Art Gallery.

BOULDER CITY/HOOVER DAM MUSEUM *1305 Arizona St. (in Boulder Dam Hotel); P.O. Box 60516, 89006. (702) 294-1988. Open daily 10 a.m.-5 p.m.; Sun. noon-5 p.m. Closed Jan. 1, Thanksgiving and Dec. 25. $1 donation; 50¢ for children.* This small museum exhibits Hoover Dam-related artifacts, including a display of a dam workers' tent-house and a variety of historical photographs.

The Boulder City Historic District preserves the atmosphere of an earlier era.

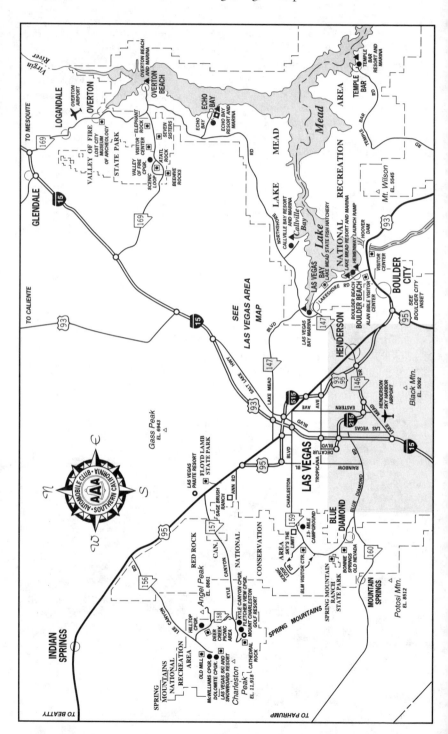

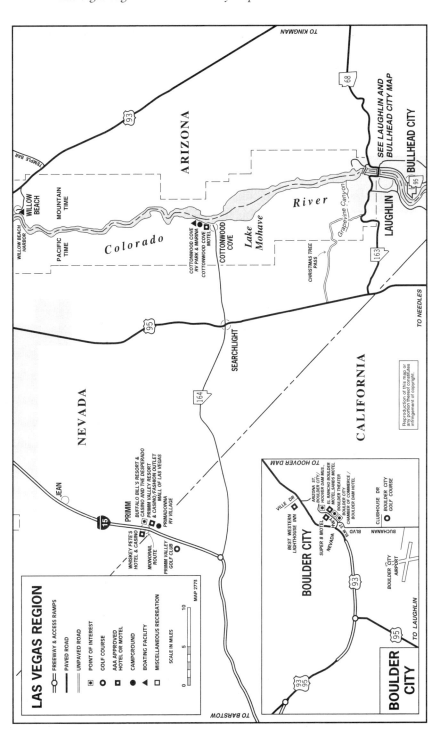

BOULDER THEATER *1225 Arizona St., 89005. Movie information, (702) 293-3145. First-run movies shown daily; call for schedule.* Opened in 1932, the Boulder Theater is the oldest movie theater in continuous operation in Nevada. The building is listed in the National Register of Historic Places.

Lake Mead National Recreation Area

HOOVER DAM *30 miles southeast of Las Vegas via US 93/95 on US 93; P.O. Box 60400, Boulder City 89006-0400. (702) 294-3523. Guided tours daily 8:30 a.m.-6:30 p.m. Closed Thanksgiving and Dec. 25. Adults, $8; ages 62 and over, $7; ages 6-16, $2; ages 5 and under, free. Hard hat tour, $25. Free parking on Ariz. side; paid parking in shelter on Nev. side.* This 726-foot-high dam is a National Historic Landmark and considered one of the engineering wonders of the world. Built during the Great Depression with the skill, long hours and dedication of thousands of construction workers, it was completed in 1935—two years ahead of schedule. Not only did the dam help control the sometimes violent Colorado River, but it provided a cheap source of electricity, which aided the development of Las Vegas and Southern California. As an additional bonus, the dam created Lake Mead, America's largest manmade reservoir and a popular recreation spot.

In 1995, a $123-million visitor center and five-story parking structure opened to the public. The three-level visitor center features an exhibit gallery, revolving theater and observation platform. Two high-speed elevators operate daily to lower visitors 520 feet into the walls of Black Canyon for a 35-minute tour of the dam's power plant; a one-hour hard hat tour provides a "behind-the-scenes" view of the structure's inner workings. For all visitors, the view from the bottom of Hoover Dam is awesome, leaving no doubt that this structure is truly an engineering marvel.

LAKE MEAD *25 miles southeast of Las Vegas.* **Alan Bible Visitor Center** *located 4 miles northeast of Boulder City on US 93. (702) 293-8990, 293-8906. The visitor center is open daily 8:30 a.m.-4:30 p.m. Closed Jan. 1, Thanksgiving and Dec. 25. Free. The 6 major recreation areas on Lake Mead are* **Boulder Beach**, *28 miles southeast via US 93 and SR 166;* **Las Vegas Bay**, *17 miles east via SR 147/Lake Mead Blvd.;* **Callville Bay**, *29 miles east via SR 147, Northshore and Callville Bay rds.;* **Echo Bay**, *54 miles northeast via SR 147, Northshore Rd. and access road to Echo Bay;* **Overton Beach**, *60 miles northeast via I-15 and SR 169; and* **Temple Bar**, *in Ariz., 75 miles southeast via US 93 and Temple Bar Rd. For emergency assistance in the Lake Mead National Recreation Area call (800) 680-5851 (911 is not fully implemented in the Lake Mead National Recreation Area).*

Lake Mead is the largest manmade reservoir in the United States. It is administered by the National Park Service as part of the Lake Mead National Recreation Area, which also includes Lake Mohave, downstream from Hoover Dam. Lake Mead is 110 miles long and has a shoreline five times that length. Created by Hoover Dam, the lake area offers year-round fishing, swimming, water-skiing, camping, hiking, picnicking, scuba diving, sailing, powerboating and houseboating. Information about the recreation area can be obtained at the Alan Bible Visitor Center on US 93, which also has a botanical garden, bookstore and exhibits on natural history.

Much of Lake Mead's surrounding landscape is rugged desert interspersed with stark grayish-purple mountains, colorful red rock canyons and a variety of desert shrubbery. Mild weather throughout most of the year is punctuated by hot, dry summers when temperatures often reach over 100 degrees. The desert environment is home to more than 1000 bighorn sheep that roam the rocky ridges, while the manmade lake attracts ducks, cormorants, geese, egrets, herons, ospreys and bald eagles.

The lake offers some of the best sportfishing in the country and an open season on all fish year round (see Water Recreation in the *Recreation* chapter). There are many **scenic drives** through this dramatic region. A popular one follows Northshore Road, running north from Lake Mead Boulevard (SR 147) to Echo Bay and Overton Beach. An often spectacular view of the surrounding mountains and hills can be seen from this route, where the browns, burnt reds and black rocks of the landscape are contrasted with the stark off-whites and tans. Each hill is seemingly formed from a different material, but all are the product of an active geologic past.

The red and black rocks that dominate the scenery speak of the high iron and magnesium content of the volcanic debris. Local sedimentary rocks, such as the sandstone layers evidenced in the nearby hills, were laid down by water and then uplifted at a later time. A high iron content is also evidenced there, often by an entire range of stark red hills. The vividness of the colors of the rocks seen on this drive can often vary not only with the time of day, but also with the direction of travel. What may appear dull and drab through the front windshield may look entirely different in the rearview mirror. Drive carefully— one of the greatest hazards here is looking at the landscape instead of the road.

Caution: Care should be taken when traveling in this area.

• Desert thunderstorms in summer and fall can produce both lightning and flash floods. Never camp in a wash or low-lying area. Never drive across

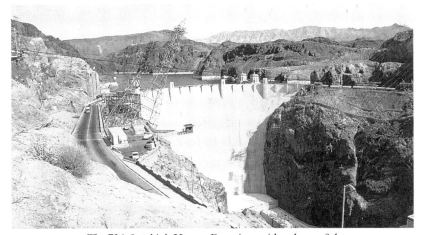

The 726-foot-high Hoover Dam is considered one of the engineering wonders of the world.

flooded roads; many roads have been posted flash-flood areas.

- Summer's extreme temperatures can cause heat exhaustion and heat stroke, as well as cripple a car that does not have adequate coolant in the cooling system. Refer to the Desert Driving Hints in the *Transportation* chapter.

- Rattlesnakes and scorpions are indigenous to this area and poisonous. They usually will not strike unless cornered, but caution should be taken to avoid them.

- Drive only on paved roads or on unpaved roads marked with yellow arrows. Check with rangers about road conditions before traveling unpaved roads.

LAKE MEAD STATE FISH HATCHERY *9½ miles north of Boulder City on SR 166/Lakeshore Rd. (702) 486-6738. Open daily 8 a.m.-4 p.m. Free.* This facility is a cold-water hatchery used for trout. Its visitor center features displays on production methods.

LAKE MOHAVE *Extends 67 miles north from Davis Dam along the Colorado River. Ranger stations can be found at the 3 major recreation areas on the lake:* **Katherine Landing**, *6 miles north of Bullhead City via SR 95, SR 68 and north on an access road; (520) 754-3272.* **Cottonwood Cove**, *55 miles north of Laughlin via Laughlin Cutoff Rd., SR 163, US 95 and an access road east from Searchlight.* **Willow Beach**, *81 miles north of Bullhead City via SR 95, SR 68 to Kingman, US 93 north and an access road west; (520) 767-4000. For general information call (702) 293-8907; for Lake Mohave weather call (702) 297-1265.*

Lake Mohave's teal waters provide a sharp contrast to the desert landscape surrounding it. Its northern section is almost as narrow as the Colorado River itself, with Indian petroglyphs etched on the steep walls of Black Canyon. The midsection widens to almost four miles before narrowing again to the south, where the shore is lined with hundreds of small coves and inlets.

The contrast of the water to the desert is also reflected in the colorful flora and fauna. The lake is an abundant source of water for traditional desert dwellers as well as a winter home for many migratory bird species. Homes for Gila monsters, scorpions, tarantulas, burros and coyotes, as well as small beavers, muskrats and bighorn sheep, can be found in the area. Birds run the gamut from hawks and large crows to roadrunners and blue heron. Spring often brings a display of wildflowers (most notably brittlebush and sand verbena) among the desert plants.

Lake Mohave is ideal for boating year round, but those pursuing land adventures will find the best months to visit are October through April. Winters are mild, with daytime temperatures generally ranging from 65 to 85 degrees. Brutally hot summers are routinely above the 100-degree mark and sometimes reach 120 degrees.

The lake's main appeal is in the variety of recreation it offers. Houseboating and fishing are popular, as are swimming, scuba diving, water-skiing, wind surfing, jet skiing and sunbathing. Houseboats can be rented at Katherine Landing and Cottonwood Cove marinas, but reservations must be made well in advance. A fish hatchery at Willow Beach supplies the rainbow trout that are planted in the lake. Lake Mohave has a reputation as one of the best trout and largemouth bass fishing areas in the Southwest.

Overton

LOST CITY MUSEUM OF ARCHEOLOGY *60 miles northeast of Las Vegas via I-15 and SR 169; 721 S. Moapa Valley Blvd.; P.O. Box 807, 89040. (702) 397-2193. Open daily 8:30 a.m.-4:30 p.m. Closed major holidays. Adults, $2; ages 17 and under, free.* This museum offers visitors a chance to see both original American Indian relics and faithful reconstructions of Pueblo dwellings. The last 10,000 years have seen several cultures in residence, including the Gypsum Cave People, ancient Basket Makers, Early Pueblos and, most recently, the Paiute Indians who came to the area about 900 years ago. Many ruins near the museum have not yet been excavated, and as the delicate process of unearthing the remains continues, more and more is revealed about the area's past inhabitants.

Primm

Located 40 miles south of Las Vegas at the California/Nevada state line on I-15, 89019. Buffalo Bill's, Primm Valley and Whiskey Pete's (702) 382-1212, (800) 386-7867. Roller coaster and Turbo Drop, $5 per person; log ride, $4 per person; motion theater, $3 per person. This area, quite literally at the California-Nevada state line, was once just a drive-through hamlet on the way to bigger and better things. It was popularly known as Stateline for several years. Today, however, Primm is itself a high-wattage destination, offering entertainment, lodging, dining and gaming at three large resort-style hotels.

At Buffalo Bill's Resort & Casino, one of tallest and fastest roller coasters in the world, the **"Desperado,"** offers thrilling rides around the entire property and into the casino itself. The roller coaster plunges 225 feet and reaches

Faithful reconstructions of Indian pueblo dwellings can be found at the Lost City Museum of Archeology in Overton.

speeds of 80 mph while riders glimpse spectacular views of the surrounding desert. Additional thrills can be had on the **Turbo Drop**, which lifts riders 200 feet above the desert and sends them down at 45 mph before bouncing gently on air brakes. A little tamer, but just as fun, is the **Water Flume Log Ride**, which crisscrosses the path of the roller coaster and finishes with a gentle ride through the casino.

A **Western-style train** links Buffalo Bill's to Primm Valley, where in between knocking down turkeys (three consecutive strikes) at the regulation bowling center, visitors can view an ornamental 100-foot **Ferris wheel** and a **merry-go-round**. Primm Valley also touts a 21,000-square-foot **convention center**.

From Primm Valley, a sleek, futuristic-looking **monorail** whisks passengers over I-15 to Whiskey Pete's Hotel & Casino. The hotel displays two classic gangster cars near the monorail terminal: the **original Bonnie and Clyde**

"Death Car" and the restored **Dutch Shultz-Al Capone Gangster Car**.

Meanwhile, Primm has shown no signs of standing pat as it continues to add new attractions. In 1997, the **Primm Valley Golf Club** opened, offering two 18-hole championship courses for duffers to champions. (See Golf in the *Recreation* chapter.) The Turbo Drop and convention center were also new additions during 1997. The **Fashion Outlet of Las Vegas**, a 400,000-square-foot outlet mall, opened in 1998 and features upscale stores from apparel companies around the world, a food court and a multilanguage concierge.

Red Rock Canyon National Conservation Area

18 miles west of Las Vegas via SR 159/W. Charleston Blvd. or 20 miles west of Las Vegas via SR 160/Blue Diamond Rd. **Visitor center** *located to*

Primm is the site of a growing number of attractions.

the left of the scenic loop drive entrance; mailing address: Bureau of Land Management, Red Rock Canyon National Conservation Area, HCR 33, Box 5500, Las Vegas 89124. (702) 363-1921. Open daily 8:30 a.m.-4:30 p.m. Closed Thanksgiving and Dec. 25. Entrance fee: $5 per vehicle; bicyclists and pedestrians, free. Just a short drive from the urban wonders of Las Vegas, Red Rock Canyon features nature at its best: a 13-mile scenic loop drive, more than 20 miles of hiking trails, horseback riding, numerous panoramic overlooks, a variety of flora and fauna, American Indian rock art, plus a well-stocked visitor center with exhibit rooms and a bookstore. Picnicking sites are located at Red Spring and Willow Spring.

Because Red Rock Canyon is higher in elevation than Las Vegas (up to 5000 feet) and has double the annual rainfall (about 8 to 12 inches), a wider variety of plant and animal life is able to flourish here. Cacti, annuals, yucca (such as the Joshua tree) and trees (ponderosa and piñon pines, juniper and willow) are prevalent, as are many types of birds, such as hawks, eagles, falcons, roadrunners, owls, ravens and wrens. Many other birds migrate through during the spring and fall; the visitor center staff can provide a complete list.

Much of the wildlife in Red Rock is visible only during the early morning and late evening hours, when cooler temperatures prevail. Night-dwellers include mule deer, coyotes, mountain lions, badgers, bobcats, jack rabbits and bats. Easier-to-spot diurnal inhabitants are bighorn sheep, wild burros, wild horses and antelope ground squirrels (identified by their white tails).

Reptiles are no strangers to the area, and include tree frogs, geckos, lizards and snakes. There are also three types of poisonous rattlesnakes here, namely the sidewinder, Mojave green and Mojave speckled. Hot days (above 70 degrees) bring out snakes; use caution when hiking. And remember, all animals (including snakes) are protected at Red Rock Canyon.

The **Scenic Loop Drive** is a convenient way to view the beauty of Red Rock Canyon; the road is located just off SR 159 and open daily from 7 a.m. to dusk. This one-way, 13-mile route begins near the visitor center, then returns to SR 159 about two miles farther south. The drive offers a close look at the area's Aztec sandstone, plant life and the **Keystone Thrust Fault**. The fault occurred some 65 million years ago and is considered the most significant geologic feature of Red Rock Canyon. It is believed that two of the Earth's crustal plates collided with such force that part of one plate was shoved up and over the younger sandstone. The thrust contact is evidenced by the sharp contrast between the gray limestone and the red sandstone.

The first two pullouts on the scenic loop have short trails to the base of the **Calico Hills**, where seasonal rain pools can be found. These pools often become temporary homes to small insects, insect larvae and fairy shrimp. Easier hiking can be found a little farther along the drive at the **Sandstone Quarry** (a short, graded dirt road leads to this spot). From the historic quarry, many small canyons can be explored. A side road leads to the Willow Spring Picnic Area and a ³/₁₀-mile hike from the road takes visitors to **Lost Creek Canyon**, the site of a year-round spring and occasional seasonal waterfall.

Farther along the gently curving drive is **Ice Box Canyon Overlook**. From this location, visitors can take a ⅖-mile hike to a box canyon surrounded by steep walls; the walls keep this canyon cooler than others in the area—hence the name. The end of the hike is reached by "boulder hopping" an additional ½ mile across the canyon bottom. Seasonal pools and an occasional waterfall can also be found here. The last stop along the road is the **Pine Creek Canyon Overlook**, one of the area's most popular hiking trails. The two-mile round trip features a running creek, ponderosa pines and the remains of a historic homestead.

The scenic loop drive is also an excellent way for experienced **bicyclists** to see the area. The one-way paved road assures riders of no oncoming traffic, and since the road is two lanes wide, there is plenty of room for cars to pass. Bicyclists will, however, find the road a bit of a challenge. Its steep, undulating grades gain 1000 feet in altitude over

the first five miles, followed by switch-backs at the top of the grade, then by a 1000-foot drop in elevation over the last eight miles. Round-trip mileage is about 15 miles. Bicyclists should beware of weekend and holiday traffic, which can be heavy, and keep a lookout for falling rocks in the switchbacks, and loose pebbles and debris where the road crosses a wash. Since there is no repair facility or air for tires available in the park or in nearby Blue Diamond, cyclists should come prepared to make their own repairs. The visitor center has a brochure detailing the route.

Safety Guidelines:

• Thunderstorms, especially in summer and early fall, can produce both lightning and flash floods. Never drive across flooded roads or cross low-lying areas when water is running.

The Scenic Loop Drive offers views of the vivid red sandstone in the Calico Hills.

- Charcoal fires are allowed at designated sites where grills are provided. Ground fires are prohibited.

- Camping is permitted only in designated locations.

- Climbing on sandstone requires equipment and experience. Sandstone is soft and crumbly and can be dangerous to climbers.

- Heat, cold and dehydration can take their toll on hikers. Carry one gallon of water for each person per day. Summer days can bring extreme heat, and temperatures drop rapidly at night.

- All natural and historic features are protected by federal law. This includes animals, plants, rocks and American Indian artifacts. Do not damage, disturb or remove them.

- Do not feed the burros at Red Rock Canyon. Feeding burros encourages them to congregate on the roads, where many have been killed or injured by vehicles. Burros have also been known to bite, kick and step out in front of cars unexpectedly. Use caution and observe them from a distance.

BONNIE SPRINGS OLD NEVADA *Off SR 159/W. Charleston Blvd., 5½ miles south of the Red Rock Canyon Visitor Center; 1 Gun Fighter Ln., 89004. (702) 875-4191. Open daily at 10:30 a.m.; during daylight-saving time to 6 p.m., standard time to 5 p.m.; tickets sold until 1 hour before closing. Petting zoo open daily at 10 a.m.; during daylight-saving time to 6 p.m., standard time to 5 p.m. Train operates Sat., Sun. and holidays only. Admission to Old Nevada: adults, $6.50; ages 62 and over, $5.50; ages 5-11, $4; train rides and petting zoo, free.* In the 1800s Bonnie Springs Ranch was a stopover for wagon trains traveling the Old Spanish Trail. In 1952, Al and Bonnie Levinson built a replica of an old western town here and fashioned it into a tourist attraction. Free activities include the petting zoo and rides on a miniature train. The petting zoo has donkeys, pigs, llamas, deer, a variety of other farm animals and a duck pond; food to feed them can be purchased from on-site vending machines. For a fee, visitors can experience the Old Nevada Village, a western-style town that offers staged gunfights and hangings, a melodrama, wax museum, blacksmith display, stagecoach rides, horseback rides and more. A western-themed motel, gift shop, restaurant and saloon are also on the premises.

SPRING MOUNTAIN RANCH STATE PARK *South of Scenic Loop Dr., off SR 159; P.O. Box 124, Blue Diamond 89004. (702) 875-4141; summer theater information (702) 594-7529. Day-use area open 8 a.m.-dusk.* **Visitor center/ranch house** *open Mon.-Fri. noon-4 p.m., Sat., Sun. and holidays 10 a.m.-4 p.m. Guided tours of the historic area Fri.-Mon. and holidays; call for schedule. Entrance fee: $5 per vehicle.* This 528-acre park at the base of the majestic Wilson Cliffs overflows with tranquil beauty. Listed on the National Register of Historic Sites, the area was once the alternate route of the Old Spanish Trail during the 1830s, a welcome oasis for weary travelers. Through most of this century the site was used as a cattle ranch, changing ownership several times (including with Howard Hughes), before coming under park protection in 1974. Tours of the historic site and its circa-1860s structures are given throughout the year. A large, grassy day-use area, shaded by scrub oak and mesquite trees, is available for picnickers; tables and barbecue grills are provided. The park hosts many activities, including musicals at its outdoor theater June through August, and living history programs in the spring and fall.

Spring Mountains National Recreation Area

35 miles northwest of Las Vegas via US 95, turnoff at SR 157/Kyle Canyon Rd. or SR 156/Lee Canyon Rd. **Visitor Center (Las Vegas)** *4 blocks west of Sahara Blvd. at 2881 S. Valley View Blvd., Ste. 16, 89102. (702) 873-8800. Open Mon.-Fri. 8 a.m.-4:30 p.m. Closed Sat., Sun. and holidays.* **Visitor center (Kyle Canyon)** *at Mile Marker 3 on SR 157. (702) 872-5486. Hours vary; call for information.* Barely a 45-minute drive from the glitz of Las Vegas is

Spring Mountains National Recreation Area. Part of the Humboldt-Toiyabe National Forest, Spring Mountains NRA provides a lush reprieve from high temperatures and stark landscapes of the desert. By taking the Spring Mountains Scenic Loop, visitors are exposed to a number of appealing sights as the road climbs to its maximum elevation of 8500 feet. At this elevation, the temperature in the forest is usually 30 degrees cooler than in Las Vegas. Weekend crowds attest to the forest's popularity; weekdays are usually quieter.

Caution: Portions of the national forest may close for the winter as early as October (depending on weather conditions), and tire chains may be required at any time during winter months. Gasoline is not available on the mountain.

Cathedral Rock, **Old Mill**, **Foxtail** and **Deer Creek** are enjoyable picnic spots. Another feature to look for is

Joshua trees line the entrance to Spring Mountain Ranch State Park.

Spring Mountains National Recreation Area offers snow sports in the winter and a lush reprieve from high desert temperatures in the summer.

Mummy Mountain, so named because it looks like a huge mummy lying on its back. Restaurant dining with outdoor seating is available near Cathedral Rock. Hikers should bring comfortable walking shoes in order to experience the area's beauty close-up; numerous hiking trails offer broad vistas and interesting flora and fauna.

Charleston Peak is the third highest peak in Nevada. A trail to the 11,918-foot summit is usually open between June and October, though weather conditions can lengthen or shorten the hiking season considerably. Hikers should be in good condition before attempting the climb; the gain in elevation from start to finish is almost 4000 feet, and the total round trip is more than 18 miles.

LAS VEGAS SKI AND SNOW-BOARD RESORT *47 miles northwest of Las Vegas via US 95 and SR 156/Lee Canyon Rd. (702) 385-2754. Open Thanksgiving to Easter, daily 9 a.m.-4 p.m.* Rentals (alpine skis, boots and poles, snowboards), snowmaking, night skiing, ski school, snack bar and day lodge are all available. Runs are 15 percent novice, 65 percent intermediate and 20 percent advanced, with the longest run being ⅜ mile. The vertical drop is 1000 feet. Three double chairs service the area; prices vary, call for information. The nearest AAA-approved accommodations are in Las Vegas. Remember that tire chains may be required when driving to this area.

Valley of Fire State Park

50 miles northeast of Las Vegas via I-15 and SR 169 (Valley of Fire Rd.); P.O. Box 515, Overton 89040. (702) 397-2088. Entrance fee: $4 per vehicle.

Camping fee: $11 per vehicle. **Visitor center** *located just off Valley of Fire Rd. midway into the park. Open daily 8:30 a.m.-4:30 p.m. Closed Jan. 1 and Dec. 25.* So named because of the effect of bright sunlight reflecting off red sandstone, Valley of Fire State Park is a visually stunning area that contains dozens of unique geological formations and remnants of an ancient American Indian civilization.

During the dinosaur age 150 million years ago, these great sandstone formations were created from shifting sand dunes and years of uplifting, faulting and erosion. Prehistoric inhabitants of the area included the Basket Maker people, and later, the Anasazi Pueblo farmers from the nearby Moapa Valley.

There are literally countless natural formations here, brilliantly red in color, and all different shapes and sizes. **Elephant Rock** is one of the most photographed, located near the east entrance station; it looks like the profile of an elephant when viewed from the hill behind, looking toward Valley of Fire Road. **Seven Sisters** is another striking formation, and easily visible from Valley of Fire Road, just east of the visitor center. **The Beehives**, weathered by wind and water, are near the west entrance station. The remnants of petrified logs are also within in the park, although thoughtless visitors have taken so many samples that the amount of petrified wood is considerably depleted.

For examples of **petroglyphs**—pictures carved into rock—**Atlatl Rock** is one of the best. Situated near the center of the park along Scenic Loop Road, the petroglyphs of the towering rock are easily viewed by walking up a steep, metal staircase. Visitors who brave the 83 mesh-covered steps to the top will be rewarded with the sight of ancient, well-preserved figures carved into the rock. Another site known for its petroglyphs is **Mouse's Tank**, a natural basin named after an early renegade who used the area as a hideout. Water collects in the rock after a rainfall, occasionally remaining in the tank for months.

Because of its rare beauty, Valley of Fire has been used many times as the background for motion pictures. There are numerous hiking trails, as well as camping and picnicking facilities. The visitor center

Elephant Rock is one of the most photographed formations in Valley of Fire State Park.

has an outdoor botanical garden, displays of local fauna, and information about the park and its hiking trails.

Caution: Care should be taken when traveling in this area.

- Thunderstorms, especially in summer and early fall, can produce both lightning and flash floods. Camp only in designated areas and never drive across flooded roads.

- All natural and historic features are protected. This includes animals, plants, rocks and American Indian artifacts. Do not damage, disturb or remove them.

- Care should be taken when hiking in canyon areas. Taking shortcuts may be dangerous. Never hike alone. Register at the visitor center before hiking backcountry areas. No overnight backpacking.

A climb to Atlatl Rock is richly rewarded with close-up views of Indian petroglyphs.

GUIDED TOURS

The tours listed in this section generally last less than a day, though some of the trips to more distant places involve an overnight stay. Be sure to contact the companies in advance for complete information and reservations, including deposit requirements and cancellation notice; scheduled tours are subject to cancellation if there is an insufficient number of passengers. Many tours offer hotel pickup and discounted children's rates.

Tours listed are provided as a convenience for our readers; inclusion in this publication does not imply endorsement by the Automobile Club of Southern California.

Boulder City

BLACK CANYON RAFT TOURS
1297 Nevada Hwy., 89005. (800) 696-7238, (702) 293-3776. Operates Feb. through Nov. Closed Dec. and Jan. Adults, $64.95; ages 5-12, $35; lunch included. Reservations advised.
Colorado River raft trips from Hoover Dam to Willow Beach.

LAKE MEAD AIR *1301 Airport Rd.; P.O. Box 60035, 89006. (702) 293-1848, 293-9906; FAX (702) 294-0232.*

Grand Canyon, Hoover Dam/Lake Mead air and air/land packages. **(See ad page 51.)**

LAKE MEAD CRUISES *P.O. Box 62465, 89006. (702) 293-6180. Midday sightseeing cruise: adults, $16; ages 2-11, $6. Fri.-Sat. evening dinner/dance cruise: adults, $43. Sun.-Thu. early dinner cruise: adults, $29; ages 2-11, $15. Sat.-Sun. breakfast cruise: adults, $21; ages 2-11, $10. Reservations recommended.* Lake Mead sternwheeler cruises depart from Lake Mead Cruises Landing.

SHOWROOM ENTERTAINMENT

Primm's showrooms, while not as pervasive nor as elaborate as those in Las Vegas, still add a noteworthy dimension to this growing tourist destination.

Tickets for shows may be purchased by phoning or visiting the hotel's showroom box office or by contacting a local ticket agency, of which there are a number that specialize in booking entertainment. Refer to the telephone directory yellow pages under "Ticket Sales/Events" or "Tourist Information."

Primm

Located along I-15 at the California-Nevada state line, this emerging area offers production shows, special events and lounge entertainment. Times and prices vary with entertainers.

BUFFALO BILL'S RESORT AND CASINO

On east side of I-15. (702) 386-7867, (800) 386-7867.

Star of the Desert Arena — Top-name entertainment and special events.

WHISKEY PETE'S HOTEL AND CASINO
On west side of I-15. (702) 386-7867,

(800) 386-7867.

Whiskey Pete's Showroom — Top-name entertainment.

A N N U A L   E V E N T S

The Boulder City area plays host to a number of annual events, while Logandale, more than 50 miles northeast of Las Vegas, hosts the Clark County Fair each year. For detailed information about each event, please call the telephone numbers shown, or consult with the local chamber of commerce or visitor information bureau.

April

CLARK COUNTY FAIR *Clark County Fairgrounds, Logandale, Nev. (702) 398-3247.* This four-day event features livestock shows, pony rides, arts and crafts booths, a PRCA rodeo, and carnival rides.

May

SPRING JAMBOREE & CRAFT FAIR *Bicentennial Park, Boulder City, Nev. (702) 293-2034.* A two-day arts and crafts fair, classic car show, food booths and music are all part of this springtime festival.

July

DAMBOREE *Boulder City, Nev. (702) 293-2034.* Fourth of July events include a parade, games, children's activities, live music, a carnival and fireworks.

September

RATTLIN' RAILS HANDCAR RACES *Boulder City, Nev. (402)* *595-7223.* Five-person teams from as far away as Canada compete in different categories over two days, racing handcars down a pair of railroad tracks. A barbecue and awards ceremony follow.

October

ART IN THE PARK *Bicentennial Park, Boulder City, Nev. (702) 294-1611.* With arts and crafts on display in more than 350 booths, this two-day show is the largest of its kind in the western United States.

December

CHRISTMAS PARADE *Boulder City, Nev. (702) 293-2034.* A Saturday morning parade down the Nevada Highway, ending at Bicentennial Park, helps celebrate the holiday season.

PARADE OF LIGHTS *Lake Mead. (702) 293-2034 (Boulder City, Nev.).* Boats ranging in size from 16 to 34-plus feet long gather on the nation's largest manmade lake to ring in the Christmas season with an evening's blaze of festive, twinkling lights.

Laughlin-Bullhead City

*Ninety miles south of Las Vegas are the booming towns of **Laughlin, Nevada**, and **Bullhead City, Arizona**. Perched on opposite banks of the Colorado River, they lack the thrill rides or go-go atmosphere of Las Vegas, but have won a large following in their own right. Laughlin alone draws nearly 5 million tourists annually, wooed by a relaxed pace, and bargain-priced lodging and meals at its riverside hotel-casinos. Seniors especially have taken to the town, where big bands and '70s, '80s and '90s popular music draw crowds into the lounge and showroom circuit. Some 10,000 to 15,000 "snowbirds" migrate from colder climes each year to make the area their winter home.*

Moreover, the region boasts many worthwhile attractions, ranging from hiking trails and Davis Dam to an antique car collection and several historic mining towns. And of course, there's abundant recreation on the Colorado River.

POINTS OF INTEREST

Attractions are listed alphabetically. Note: The State of Arizona does not observe daylight-saving time; Mountain Standard Time is in effect year round.

COLORADO RIVER MUSEUM *On the Arizona side of the river on SR 95, ½ mile north of the Laughlin Bridge; P.O. Box 1599, Bullhead City 86430. (520) 754-3399. Open 9 a.m.-2:30 p.m. (Arizona time); Nov. through Mar. daily; Apr. through Oct. Tue.-Sat. Closed Jan. 1, Jul., Aug., Thanksgiving, Dec. 25. Donation.* Housed in a former Catholic church built in 1947 during the Davis Dam construction, this small museum features a model of Fort Mohave in the late 1800s, geologic maps of the area, a model railroad that depicts the mid 1800s, and historical photographs. Items donated to the museum include a steamboat anchor, mining tools, antique barbed wire, American Indian artifacts, a dinosaur footprint, and a piano that was shipped around Cape Horn 130 years ago.

DAVIS CAMP COUNTY PARK *On the Arizona side of the river on SR 95, ½ mile north of the Laughlin Bridge; P.O. Box 2078, Bullhead City 86430. (520)* *754-4606. Open 24 hours; day use ends at 8 p.m. $3 entrance fee, $5 holiday weekends.* The park offers a stretch of sandy beach for swimming and fishing, or launching personal watercraft, inner tubes, rafts or rubber boats. The area from the park north to Davis Dam is noted for its excellent striped bass and rainbow trout fishing. Visitors have found that a hike into the park's south section can provide views of a variety of birds and small wildlife. Camping is permitted in an RV park and along the river (see *Campgrounds & Trailer Parks*); fishing requires a license (see Water Recreation under *Recreation*).

DAVIS DAM *2 miles north of Laughlin via Casino Dr. and SR 163; U.S. Bureau of Reclamation, Davis Dam, Bullhead City 86429. (520) 754-3628.* The dam, designed to help regulate the delivery of water to the lower Colorado River region and Mexico, is a rock-fill and earthen structure augmented by concrete intakes and spill-

Several Laughlin hotels boast their own boat docks.

ways. In addition to its importance for flood control, the dam provides hydroelectric power for regional industry and irrigation for farming. The powerhouse is no longer open for tours, but the dam can still be viewed up close.

DON LAUGHLIN'S RIVERSIDE RESORT HOTEL & CASINO *1650 S. Casino Dr., Laughlin; P.O. Box 500, 89029.*

Don Laughlin's Classic Car Collection *(702) 298-2535, ext. 5678 or 5103. Open daily at 9 a.m.; Mon.-Fri. to 10 p.m., Sat. and Sun. to 11 p.m. Free.* The collection features antique, classic and futuristic "concept" automobiles from the Imperial Palace in Las Vegas and Don Laughlin's private collection. The cars are exhibited in two rooms: a

glass-walled room facing Casino Drive and the Exhibition Hall on the third floor of the hotel's new 28-story tower.

U.S.S. *Riverside (702) 298-2535, ext. 5770, (800) 227-3849, ext. 5770. Departures from Don Laughlin's Riverside boat dock. Ticket booth located on the ground level of hotel, next to boat dock.* Boat tours of the Laughlin-Bullhead City area and Davis Dam. Weddings held aboard.

Davis Dam spans the Colorado River near Laughlin.

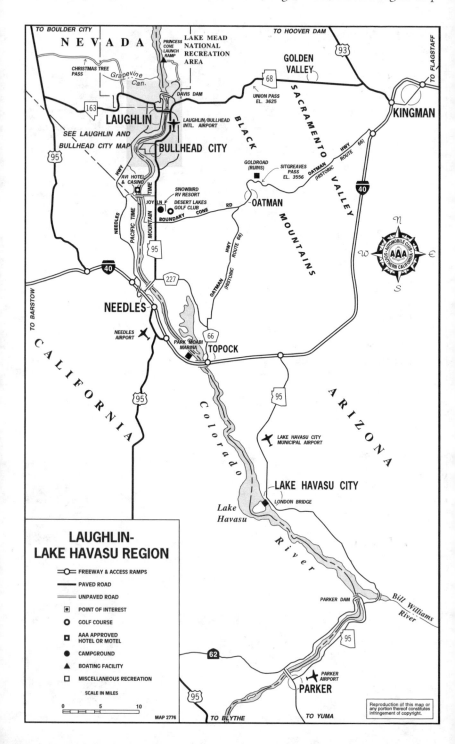

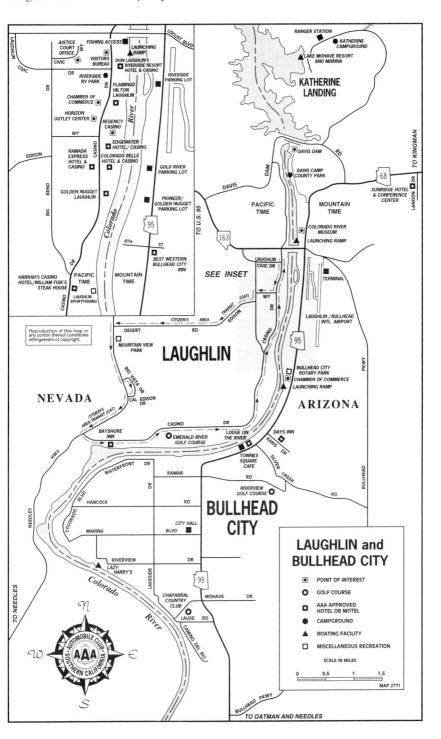

LAUGHLIN and BULLHEAD CITY

- ▣ POINT OF INTEREST
- ○ GOLF COURSE
- ▱ AAA APPROVED HOTEL OR MOTEL
- ● CAMPGROUND
- ▲ BOATING FACILITY
- ☐ MISCELLANEOUS RECREATION

SCALE IN MILES

0   0.5   1   1.5

MAP 2771

▼ *A Quick Guide to Laughlin-Bullhead City*

Population

Bullhead City	28,535
Laughlin	8,500

Elevation

Bullhead City	540 ft.
Laughlin	510 ft.

Emergency   911

Highway Conditions

Arizona	(520) 779-2711
Nevada	(702) 486-3116

Time/Weather

Arizona		(520) 763-3000
Nevada	time	(702) 844-1212
	weather	(702) 248-4800

Emergency Road Service for AAA Members

(800) AAA-HELP (in the USA and Canada)

(800) 955-4TDD (for the hearing impaired)

Newspapers

The Laughlin-Bullhead City area's daily newspaper is the *Mohave Valley Daily News* and the *Arizona Republic*. The major weeklies are the *Bullhead City Bee*, the *Weekender* and the *Laughlin Nevada Times*.

Radio Stations

Classic Rock: KLUK (108 FM); **Contemporary Rock:** KZUL (95.3 FM), KZZZ (100.3 FM); **Country:** KFLG (102.7 FM and 1000 AM), KGMN (104.7 FM), KWAZ (97.9 FM); **News/Talk:** KATO (1230 AM); **Oldies:** KRCY (105.9 FM).

TV Stations

In Laughlin, the major television stations include channels 3 (NBC), 5 (FOX), 8 (ABC) and 13 (CBS). In Bullhead City, Ariz., the major network programs appear on channels 5 (CBS), 10 (FOX), 12 (NBC) and 13 (ABC). For a complete list of television programs, consult the daily newspaper or hotel listings.

Public Transportation

Shuttles and Ferries—All of the hotels in Laughlin have large on-site parking lots. A **water taxi** runs between the casino docks at the Riverside, Edgewater, Pioneer, Golden Nugget and Harrah's; the fare is $2 one way and $3 round trip. On those occasions when the water level of the river (controlled by Davis Dam) is too low for the taxis to travel safely, parking lot pickups are made by shuttle buses.

In addition, Citizen Area Transit (CAT) operates a 24-hour **bus route** in Laughlin, covering the business district and residential area. The fare for those 18 and over is $1.50, and

75¢ for ages 65 and older and 5 to 17.

Taxi—Laughlin and Bullhead City both have taxi service, but the Arizona-based taxi companies are not allowed to operate in Nevada unless called to take a passenger from Laughlin into the state of Arizona; they are not allowed to take passengers from one casino to another or from one location in Nevada to another.

The Laughlin taxi company charges a base fare of $2.20 plus $1.50 for each mile; 30¢ per minute waiting time. Rates are unregulated for cabs operating in Bullhead City, so fares vary by company.

Laughlin

Desert	(702) 298-7575
Lucky	(702) 298-2299

Bullhead City

Bullhead City Taxi	(520) 754-7433
Lucky	(520) 754-1100
Mohave	(520) 754-4444
Tri-State	(520) 758-1024

Hospitals

Western Arizona Regional Medical Center
2735 Silver Creek Rd.
Bullhead City, AZ 86442
(520) 763-2273

Mohave Valley Hospital and Medical Center
1225 E. Hancock Rd.
Bullhead City, AZ 86442
(520) 758-3931

Laughlin Medical Center
150 E. Edison Way
Laughlin, NV 89029
(702) 298-3364

AAA/California State Automobile Association

Henderson District Office
601 Whitney Ranch Dr., Ste. A
Henderson, NV 89014
(702) 458-2323
Office hours: Mon.-Fri. 8:30 a.m.-5:30 p.m.

Las Vegas District Office
3312 W. Charleston Blvd.
Las Vegas, NV 89102
(702) 870-9171
Office hours: Mon.-Fri. 8:30 a.m.-5:30 p.m.

Summerlin
8440 W. Lake Mead Blvd., Ste. 203
(702) 360-3151
Office Hours: Mon.-Fri. 8:30 a.m.-5:30 p.m.

Visitor Services

Bullhead Area Chamber of Commerce
1251 Hwy. 95
Bullhead City, AZ 86429
(520) 754-4121
Office hours: Mon.-Fri. 9 a.m.-5 p.m., Sat. 10 a.m.-2 p.m.

Laughlin Visitors Bureau
1555 Casino Dr.
P.O. Box 502
Laughlin, NV 89029
(702) 298-3321, (800) 452-8445
Office hours: Open daily 8 a.m.-5 p.m.

**GRAPEVINE CANYON/CHRIST-
MAS TREE PASS** *7 miles west of
Davis Dam on SR 163 (about 6 miles
west of Casino Dr.), north on dirt access
road (a small sign indicates the turn).
(520) 754-3272.* This canyon offers
excellent viewing of American Indian
rock carvings of animals, fertility symbols and spiritual signs. These petroglyphs, which vary in age from 150 to
more than 600 years old, are reached
by a half-mile path from the parking
area. Hikers will travel along the edge
of a wash to a small incline in the
canyon. Primitive restrooms are available at the parking lot and hikers must
bring their own drinking water.

Heading north from the Grapevine
Canyon parking lot (toward US 95)
leads to Christmas Tree Pass, which
gets its name from the piñon and
juniper trees that locals have decorated
with ribbons, plastic lids, paper and
other bits of "trash" for many years.
About four miles out of Grapevine
Canyon the wide, graded dirt road nar-
rows considerably to allow access for
only one car in each direction; this section is not recommended for RVs. As

the road leaves Christmas Tree Pass it
widens out again for another five miles
to US 95. *Note:* This road is subject to
heavy washout during periods of rain.

Four-wheel-drive enthusiasts will find
several backcountry roads that the
National Park Service has approved for
public access. They lead to secluded
coves on the lake or into the desert
mountain backcountry. It is advisable
to check with the ranger for information about road conditions.

Caution: Flash flooding can occur
during inclement weather and sudden
summer thunderstorms. Watch for
unfenced mine shafts and pits. Stay
out of abandoned mines; deep shafts,
rotten timbers, and flammable or
poisonous gases can be concealed inside
the tunnels.

HORIZON OUTLET CENTER
*Corner of Casino Drive and Edison
Way, at 1955 S. Casino Dr, Laughlin,
Nev., 89029. (702) 298-3003. Open
daily; Mon.-Sat. 9 a.m.-8 p.m., Sun 10
a.m.-6 p.m.* This 258,000-square-foot
indoor mall has more than 60 factory
outlet stores, a food court and a movie

Historic Route 66 offers spectacular mountain scenery near Oatman.

Among Oatman's residents are wild burros that regularly roam the streets.

theater. The complex features Art Deco design throughout.

OATMAN *23 miles southeast of Bullhead City, Ariz. via SR 95 and Boundary Cone Rd., on historic Route 66 (Oatman Hwy.). (520) 768-6222.* Located in the rugged Black Mountains between Kingman and Bullhead City on historic Route 66, Oatman is an old mining town that is still brimming with the fervor of the Old West. Many of the original buildings are still in use, housing tourist-oriented enterprises, as well as a post office and several Western-style restaurants and saloons.

A prosperous gold-mining community from 1906 to 1942, local mines yielded nearly $36 million in gold at the peak of production. It was the onset of World War II that led to the town's demise, when Congress halted all mining not essential to the war effort.

Today Oatman has about 150 residents, down from a whopping 10,000 during its heyday in the 1930s. Oatman's fortuitous position along the original Route 66 (US 66) from Chicago to Los Angeles has undoubtedly helped preserve it; this town was an important last stop for travelers before entering the Mojave Desert into California.

A number of Wild West-style attractions can be seen here, including the staged daily **gunfights**; the Oatman Jail; the historic Oatman Hotel (where movie legends Clark Gable and Carole Lombard spent their wedding night in 1939); and the town's unofficial reception committee of **wild burros**. These cute, dusty animals are descendants of the burros miners turned loose years ago. They freely roam the streets in search of carrot handouts, a snack that can be purchased in local stores.

For an interesting **scenic drive** take historic Route 66 (Oatman Highway) northeast out of Oatman to Kingman. The road goes past the abandoned mining camp of **Goldroad**, climbs to the summit of the Black Mountains, then crosses the wide Sacramento Valley to **Kingman**. At times the road becomes a series of narrow hairpin curves as it winds its way up to the pass. But those with an adventurous spirit will be rewarded with panoramic views of Arizona and Nevada (maybe even California on a clear day) from the tri-state lookout point just before the summit of Sitgreaves Pass. From here, descend the eastern slope of the Black Mountains into the Sacramento Valley, an area populated with creosote bushes, yucca plants and, in season, a sprinkling of wildflowers. For the return to the Laughlin Bridge, take SR 68 west from Kingman across the flat Sacramento Valley, through a pass at the north end of the Black Mountains and down into the Colorado River Valley back to the bridge. Total mileage (from Oatman) is 60 miles. *Note:* This trip is not recommended for large RVs or trailers.

Caution: When exploring near these areas, a four-wheel-drive vehicle is recommended for travel on unpaved roads. Flash flooding can occur during summer thunderstorms, and heavy rains are possible in any season. When exploring old gold camps, watch out for unfenced mine shafts and pits. Never enter abandoned mines; deep shafts, rotted timbers, and flammable or poisonous gases can be concealed in the tunnels.

RAMADA EXPRESS HOTEL & CASINO *2121 South Casino Dr.; P.O. Box 77771, 89028.*

Gambling Train of Laughlin *Open daily; Sun-Thu. 11 a.m.-7 p.m., Fri.-Sat. 10 a.m.-10 p.m. Free.* This narrow-gauge train offers rides (but no gambling) around the parking lot of this railroad-themed hotel. The locomotive is a replica of the Genoa, an 1890's-era steam engine that hauled freight and passengers on the Virginia and Truckee line in western Nevada. Adjacent is the Great Train Store, a gift and souvenir shop for railroad enthusiasts.

GUIDED TOURS

The tours listed in this section generally last less than a day, though some of the trips to more distant places involve an overnight stay. Be sure to contact the companies in advance for complete information and reservations; many tours offer hotel pickup and discounted children's rates. Scheduled tours are subject to cancellation if there is an insufficient number of passengers.

Tours listed are provided as a convenience for our readers; inclusion in this publication does not imply an endorsement by the Automobile Club of Southern California.

DEL RIO YACHT Harrah's Casino Hotel, 2900 W. Casino Dr., 89029. (800) 742-3224. Departures from Harrah's Casino Hotel boat dock. Tickets available at dock. Boat tours of the Laughlin-Bullhead City area and Davis Dam.

LAUGHLIN RIVER TOURS, INC. *P.O. Box 29279, 89028. (702) 298-1047,*

(800) 228-9825. Depending on cruise, departures at Edgewater, Flamingo Hilton or River Palms boat docks. Tickets available at docks of all 3 hotels. Laughlin-Bullhead City area tours take place aboard a paddle-wheel boat.

U.S.S. RIVERSIDE—See Don Laughlin's Riverside Resort Hotel & Casino.

SHOWROOM ENTERTAINMENT

Laughlin does not offer the elaborate, long-running stage shows for which Las Vegas is famous. But its showrooms, cabarets and lounges do offer a variety of entertainment ranging from headline performers to lounge acts. While the facilities listed here seat 500 or more, many smaller venues are popular as well. Showroom listing does not imply AAA endorsement for the lodging establishment. For the most current information, refer to the Auto Club's "Las Vegas Shows" schedule, available to AAA members at all district offices.

Lounge entertainment is available at all of the casinos, although some do not offer shows on Monday. The Riverside's Western Ballroom on the second floor of the hotel's south tower features a tea dance every Sunday from 2 to 6 p.m.; reservations are not needed. In the evenings, the ballroom features live country music and dancing on its 1400-square-foot dance floor. Also, the Ramada Express offers dance contests Tuesday through Saturday at 4 p.m. in the Caboose Lounge. Times and prices vary with entertainers.

DON LAUGHLIN'S RIVERSIDE RESORT HOTEL & CASINO
1650 S. Casino Dr. (702) 298-2535, ext. 616, (800) 227-3849.

Don's Celebrity Theatre — *Reservations recommended.* Top-name entertainment.

FLAMINGO HILTON-LAUGHLIN
1900 S. Casino Dr. (702) 298-5111, (800) 435-8469.

Amphitheatre — *Outdoor seating in spring and fall.* Top-name entertainment.

Silver Bullet Showroom — "Dancin' to the Hitz" (Indefinitely). *Sat.-Thu. 7:30 and 9:30 p.m. Dark Fri. $9.95 per person.*

RIVER PALMS RESORT CASINO
2700 S. Casino Dr. (702) 298-2242, (800) 835-7904.

Bermuda Club — Top-name entertainment.

HARRAH'S CASINO HOTEL
2900 W. Casino Dr. (702) 298-4600.

Fiesta Showroom — Top-name entertainment.

Rio Vista Outdoor Amphitheater— Top name entertainment.

RAMADA EXPRESS HOTEL & CASINO
2121 S. Casino Dr. (702) 298-4200; (800) 243-6846.

Pavilion Showroom – Top-name entertainment and "On the Wings of Eagles" (Indefinitely). *Daily 9 a.m.-4 p.m. on the hour. Free.* A tribute to the men and women who served in our armed forces from World War II through Desert Storm is projected simultaneously on four movie screens.

ANNUAL EVENTS

Car and motorcycle rallies, rodeos, fireworks displays and even a sidewalk egg fry are among the many annual community events that Laughlin and environs have to offer. For detailed information about each event, please call the telephone numbers shown, or consult with the local chamber of commerce or visitor information bureau.

In addition, casino tournaments take place in many Laughlin area casinos. Anyone interested in these tournaments should contact the hotel or venue directly for dates and play information; room reservations should be made well in advance, as room space is often at a premium during a tournament.

January

DOWNHILL BED RACES
Oatman, Ariz. (520) 768-6222. During mid-January, five-person teams push old iron beds to the finish line on a downhill, zigzag race course.

LAUGHLIN DESERT CHALLENGE *Starts and finishes at corner of Big Bend Dr. and Edison Wy., Laughlin, Nev. (702) 298-2214, (800) 227-5245.* More than 200 of the world's top drivers compete over two days in an off-road race through the rough terrain outside of Laughlin.

TURQUOISE CIRCUIT FINALS RODEO *Corner of Marina Blvd. and Hwy. 95, Bullhead City, Ariz. (520) 754-4121.* This PRCA-sanctioned event features three days of calf-roping, bareback bull and bronco riding, music, food and vendor booths.

March

SILVERY COLORADO RIVER ROCK CLUB GEMBOREE
Bullhead City Jr. High School, Bullhead City, Ariz. (520) 763-8271. Some years takes place in Apr. This two-day event features displays of rocks, including rocks for purchase, and demonstrations of lapidary, jewelry, minerals, faceting and a silent auction.

April

DESERT TWIRLERS JAMBOREE
Mohave High School, Bullhead City, Ariz. (520) 763-3424. This two-day event features square and round dancing, plus daytime workshops.

LAUGHLIN RIVER RUN
Casino Dr., Laughlin, Nev. (800) 227-5245, (702) 298-2214. This four-day motorcycle rally features Harley-Davidsons and is billed as the west coast's largest motorcycle event. Vendor booths sport a wide range of merchandise, such as motorcycle accessories, silver and turquoise jewelry, and leather apparel. Live entertainment and food are also featured.

RODEO DAYS *Casino Dr., Laughlin, Nev. (702) 298-2214, (800) 227-5245.* More than 500 participants compete for prize money in eight traditional rodeo events. Entertainment, vendor

booths, country-western dances and festivities are part of the fun and take place at area resorts and hotels.

June

RIVER DAYS *Colorado Riverfront, Laughlin, Nev. (702) 298-2214, (800) 227-5245.* Amateur and professional riders compete over three days in personal watercraft races on the Colorado River along the Laughlin shoreline. An exposition showcases the latest in personal watercraft equipment and accessories.

July

FOURTH OF JULY FESTIVITIES *Various locations. (702) 298-2214 (Laughlin, Nev.), (520) 754-4121 (Bullhead City, Ariz.), (520) 768-8070 (Oatman, Ariz.).* Independence Day is celebrated in a wide range of community events.

OATMAN SIDEWALK EGG FRY *Oatman, Ariz. (520) 768-6222.* This annual Fourth of July event features an egg and spoon race, traditional sidewalk egg fry, egg toss and chicken leg contest.

September

OATMAN GOLD CAMP DAYS *Oatman, Ariz. (520) 768-6222.* The internationally famous Burro Biscuit Throwing Contest is the highlight of this Labor Day weekend event. Other activities include a crazy hat contest, chili cookoff and barbecue.

RODDIN' ON THE RIVER *Don Laughlin's Riverside Resort Hotel & Casino, Laughlin, Nev. (520) 754-5112.* Hot rods, classic customs and mini trucks are showcased during this four-day event. Highlights include slow drags and valve-cover races, and competitions for prizes.

October

COOL RIVER NITES *Various areas throughout Laughlin. (800) 452-8445.* Car enthusiasts come together for a weekend of classic '50s and '60s auto appreciation and competition. A dance, car auction and live music round out the weekend's festivities.

December

CHRISTMAS BUSH FESTIVAL *Oatman, Ariz. (520) 768-6222.* Shopkeepers and residents spend a day decorating bushes for the holidays along historic Route 66 leading into Oatman from the west.

PARADE OF LIGHTS *Katherine Landing, Ariz. (520) 754-3245.* Boats gather on Lake Mohave to celebrate the Christmas season with an evening's blaze of festive, twinkling lights.

NEW YEAR'S EVE CELEBRATIONS *(702) 298-2214 (Laughlin, Nev.), (520) 754-4121 (Bullhead City, Ariz.).* Traditional New Year's Eve festivities take place on both sides of the Colorado River.

Recreation

*With an average of nearly 300 sunny days a year, **Las Vegas** and the **Laughlin-Bullhead City** areas are ideal spots for outdoor sports. Not only are there acres of lush green golf courses, tennis courts and seemingly endless swimming pools, but the canyons and mountains offer horseback riding amid dramatic backdrops, and the **Lake Mead National Recreation Area** provides year-round boating, fishing, water-skiing and more.*

Golfing

Golf is one of the principal outdoor attractions in Las Vegas, as well as a popular sport in Laughlin-Bullhead City. Las Vegas features several championship courses, some of which host PGA and LPGA tournaments, plus several less demanding courses where the weekend golfer can enjoy a quick round. The desert climate offers nearly ideal playing conditions all year, with the exception of very high midday temperatures in July and August. In summer, golfers should arrange an early starting time to avoid the extreme heat.

Public, semi-private and private courses are listed alphabetically by city. Information given for each course includes its name, location, street address, phone number, yardage, par, slope, USGA ratings (from the preferred tee of the course), greens fees and facilities. Greens fees are given for weekday and weekend play during peak season. Some courses may not allow walking so the greens fee includes the *mandatory* golf cart fee. Some courses have senior citizen rates; call for information. Unless otherwise stated, each course is open daily.

Military golf courses listed in this publication include a phone number; call for information about play. Nine-hole courses may show par, slope and USGA rating that reflect nine holes played twice with two separate tees, or *two tees*. It follows that many 9-hole courses

may list 18-hole fees because they require 18 holes of play.

All semi-private and private courses have restrictions on public play ranging from members and guests only to liberal reciprocal agreements with members of other courses. Information on private courses is not listed, but a telephone number is provided for obtaining information about reciprocal play. As it is impossible to list all of the restrictions for each course, telephoning the course is highly recommended in lieu of knowing a member. Reservations are advised at most courses; some country clubs require reservations months in advance.

Information in this section is published as it is received from the individual courses. The listings have been made as complete as possible.

Boulder City

BOULDER CITY GOLF COURSE Public
Southeast of US 93 off Buchanan Blvd.; 1 Clubhouse Dr., 89005. (702) 293-9236. Daily rate: $27. The course is 18 holes; 6200 yards; par 72; 103 slope; 70.8 rating. Clubhouse, golf shop, professional, power carts, rental clubs, driving range; coffee shop, snack bar.

Henderson

BLACK MOUNTAIN GOLF AND COUNTRY CLUB Semi-Private
½ mile southwest of US 93 (Boulder Hwy.); 500 Greenway Rd., 89015. (702)

565-7933. *Closed Dec. 25. Rates including golf cart: Mon.-Thu. $55, Fri.-Sun. $60.* The course is 18 holes; 6550 yards; par 72; 120 slope; 69.8 rating. Clubhouse, locker room, golf shop, professional, power carts, rental clubs, driving range; restaurant, coffee shop, snack bar.

THE LEGACY GOLF CLUB Public
North of SR 146 (Lake Mead Dr.) off N. Green Valley Pkwy.; 130 Par Excellence Dr., 89014. (702) 897-2187. Closed Dec. 25. Rate including mandatory golf cart: Mon.-Thu. $115, Fri.-Sun. $125. The course is 18 holes; 6211 yards; par 72; 118 slope; 69.1 rating. Clubhouse, golf shop, professional, power carts, rental clubs, driving range; restaurant, snack bar.

WILDHORSE GOLF CLUB Public
3 miles west of US 95 via Sunset Rd. and Green Valley Pkwy.; 1 Showboat Country Club Dr., 89014. (702) 434-9009. Rates including mandatory golf cart: Mon.-Thu. $70-110, Fri.-Sun. $85-135. The course is 18 holes; 6461 yards; par 72; 124 slope; 69.7 rating. Golf shop, professional, power carts, rental clubs, driving range; restaurant, snack bar.

Las Vegas

ANGEL PARK GOLF CLUB Public
5 miles west of SR 95 off Summerlin Pkwy.; 100 S. Rampart Blvd., 89128. (702) 254-4653. Closed Dec. 25. Please call for daily rates. The **Mountain Course** is 18 holes; 6722 yards; par 71; 128 slope; 72.4 rating. The **Palm Course** is 18 holes; 6530 yards; par 70; 129 slope; 70.9 rating. Clubhouse, locker room, golf shop, professional, power carts, rental clubs, driving range,

night lighting for courses and driving range; restaurant, snack bar.

BADLANDS GOLF CLUB Public
3½ miles west of US 95 via Summerlin Pkwy. off Rampart Blvd.; 9115 Alta Dr., 89128. (702) 242-4653. Daily rate including mandatory golf cart: $100-160. The course is 18 holes; 6500 yards; par 72; 113 slope; 67.8 rating. Clubhouse, driving range, golf shop, professional, power carts, rental clubs; coffee shop, restaurant, snack bar.

Golf is a popular pastime at Las Vegas' numerous courses.

CANYON GATE COUNTRY CLUB Private
(702) 363-0303.

CRAIG RANCH GOLF COURSE Public
3 miles north off I-15/US 93; 628 W. Craig Rd., 89030. (702) 642-9700. Daily rate: $16. The course is 18 holes; 6001 yards; par 70; 105 slope; 66.8 rating. Clubhouse, golf shop, professional, power carts, rental clubs, driving range; snack bar.

DESERT INN GOLF CLUB Semi-Private
¾ mile east of I-15 off Flamingo Rd.; 3145 Las Vegas Blvd. S., 89109. (702) 733-4290. Daily nonhotel guest rates

including mandatory golf cart: $215.
The course is 18 holes; 7193 yards; par
72; 124 slope; 73.9 rating. Clubhouse,
locker room, golf shop, professional,
power carts, rental clubs, driving range;
tennis, swimming; restaurant, coffee
shop, snack bar.

DESERT PINES GOLF CLUB
Public
Just north of US 95 via Eastern Ave.;
3415 E. Bonanza Rd., 89101. (702)
388-4400; reservations (888) 397-2499.
Rates including mandatory golf cart:
Mon.-Thu. $65-115, Fri.-Sun. $75-135.
The course is 18 holes; 6464 yards; par
71; 122 slope; 70.4 rating. Clubhouse,
golf shop, professional, power carts,
rental clubs, driving range, night lighting for driving range; cocktail lounge,
restaurant, snack bar.

DESERT ROSE GOLF COURSE
Public
6 miles east of I-15 off Sahara Ave.;
5483 Clubhouse Dr., 89122. (702) 431-
4653. Daily rate: Mon.-Thu. $65; Fri.-
Sun. $75. The course is 18 holes; 6511
yards; par 71; 119 slope; 69.6 rating.
Clubhouse, golf shop, professional,
power carts, rental clubs, driving range;
restaurant, snack bar.

HIGHLAND FALLS GOLF
COURSE Semi-Private
10 miles northwest of downtown off Lake
Mead Blvd.; 10201 Sun City Blvd.,
89134. (702) 254-7010. Daily rate
including mandatory golf cart: $54-96.
The course is 18 holes; 6017 yards; par
72; 116 slope; 68.6 rating. Clubhouse,
golf shop, professional, power carts,
rental clubs, driving range, night lighting for driving range; coffee shop,
restaurant, snack bar.

LAS VEGAS COUNTRY CLUB
Private
(702) 734-1122.

LAS VEGAS GOLF CLUB Public
1½ miles north of US 95 via Decatur
Blvd.; 4300 Washington Ave., 89107.
(702) 646-3003. Daily rate: $59. The
course is 18 holes; 6337 yards; par 72;
114 slope; 70.3 rating. Golf shop, professional, power carts, rental clubs, driving range, night lighting for driving
range; snack bar.

LAS VEGAS NATIONAL GOLF
CLUB Public
3 miles east of I-15 via Flamingo Rd.
and Maryland Pkwy.; 1911 E. Desert
Inn Rd., 89109. (702) 734-1796. Rates
including mandatory golf cart: Mon.-
Thu. $105-125, Fri.-Sun. $144-160.
The course is 18 holes; 6418 yards; par
71; 121 slope; 70.2 rating. Clubhouse,
locker room, golf shop, professional,
power carts, rental clubs, driving range,
night lighting for driving range; restaurant, snack bar.

LAS VEGAS PAIUTE RESORT
Public
18 miles northwest of downtown off US
95 at Exit 95 (Snow Mountain), 1½
miles east to 10325 Nu-Wav Kaiv Blvd.,
89124. (702) 658-1400. Two courses;
rates for both including mandatory golf
cart: daily $125. The **Snow Mountain
Course** is 18 holes; 6035 yards; par
72; 112 slope; 68.6 rating. The **Sun
Mountain Course** is 18 holes; 6074
yards; par 72; 116 slope; 68.6 rating.
Clubhouse, golf shop, professional,
power carts, rental clubs, driving range;
banquet facilities, cigar lounge, restaurant, shop, snack bar.

LOS PRADOS GOLF COURSE
Public
On Lone Mountain Rd. and Los Prados
Blvd.; 5150 Los Prados Cir., 89130.
(702) 645-5696. Closed Dec. 25. Rates:
Mon.-Thu. $30, Fri.-Sun. and holidays
$45. The course is 18 holes; 5350

yards; par 70; 107 slope; 65.8 rating. Clubhouse, locker room, golf shop, professional, power carts, rental clubs; restaurant, coffee shop, snack bar.

NORTH LAS VEGAS COMMUNITY 3 PAR GOLF COURSE Public
1 mile west of I-15 off Cheyenne Ave.; 324 E. Brooks Ave., 89036. (702) 633-1833. Rates: Mon.-Fri. $5-6.50, Sat.-Sun. and holidays $6.50-7.50. The course is 9 holes; 1128 yards; par 27; N/A slope; N/A rating. Clubhouse, rental clubs, driving range, night lighting; coffee shop, snack bar.

PAINTED DESERT GOLF COURSE Public
¼ mile west of US 95 (Tonopah Hwy.) off Ann Rd.; 5555 Painted Mirage Wy., 89129. (702) 645-2568. Rates including mandatory golf cart: Mon.-Thu. $53-100, Fri.-Sun. $70-140. The course is 18 holes; 6323 yards; par 72; 128 slope; 71.0 rating. Clubhouse, golf shop, professional, power carts, rental clubs, driving range; restaurant, snack bar.

PALM VALLEY GOLF CLUB Semi-Private
10 miles northwest of downtown off Lake Mead Blvd.; 9201-B Del Webb Blvd., 89128. (702) 363-4373. Daily rate including mandatory golf cart: $96. The course is 18 holes; 6800 yards; par 72; 127 slope; 72.3 rating. Clubhouse, golf shop, professional, power carts, rental clubs, driving range; restaurant, snack bar.

SUNRISE VISTA GOLF COURSE Military
(702) 652-2602.

STALLION MOUNTAIN COUNTRY CLUB Private
(702) 456-3160.

TOURNAMENT PLAYERS CLUB AT SUMMERLIN Private
(702) 256-0111.

TOURNAMENT PLAYERS CLUB AT THE CANYONS Public
4 miles west of US 95 off Summerlin Pkwy., Town Center and Village Center drs. at 9851 Canyon Run Dr. (702) 256-2000. Rates including mandatory golf cart: Mon.-Wed. $140, Thu.-Sun. $170. The course is 18 holes; 6772 yards; par 71; 128 slope; 70.9 rating. Host of the Senior PGA Tour. Clubhouse, locker room, golf shop, professional, power carts, rental clubs, driving range; restaurant, snack bar.

Laughlin-Bullhead City

CHAPARRAL COUNTRY CLUB Public
7 miles south of Laughlin Bridge via SR 95; 1260 Mohave Dr., Bullhead City, AZ 86442. (520) 758-6330, (520) 758-3939. Closed Dec. 25. Daily. Please call for rates. The course is 9 holes; 2306 yards; par 32; 100 slope; 62.1 rating. Clubhouse, golf shop, professional, power carts, rental clubs; snack bar.

DESERT LAKES GOLF CLUB Public
13 miles south of Laughlin Bridge via SR 95, east on Joy Ln.; 5835 Desert Lakes Dr., Bullhead City, AZ 86430. (520) 768-1000. Winter rates including mandatory golf cart: Mon.-Thu. $57.75, Fri.-Sun. $63; call for summer, senior and twilight rates. The course is 18 holes; 6569 yards; par 72; 119 slope; 70.5 rating. Clubhouse, golf shop, professional, power carts, rental clubs, driving range; coffee shop.

EMERALD RIVER GOLF COURSE Public
1½ miles east of Needles Hwy.; 1155 S. Casino Dr., Laughlin, NV 89028. (702) 298-0061. Rates including mandatory golf cart: Mon.-Thu. $65; Fri.-Sun. $75.

The course is 18 holes; 5918 yards; par 72; 131 slope; 73.6 rating. Clubhouse, coffee shop, golf shop, professional, power carts, rental clubs, driving range; snack bar.

RIVERVIEW GOLF COURSE
Public
5 miles south of Laughlin Bridge via SR 95, east to 2000 E. Ramar Rd., Bullhead City, AZ 86442. (520) 763-1818. Winter rates: Daily $15 (9 holes) and $22 (18 holes). Call for summer rates. The course is 9 holes; 1160 yards; par 27; N/A rating. Clubhouse, golf shop, professional, hand carts, power carts, rental clubs.

Primm

PRIMM VALLEY GOLF CLUB
Public
35 miles south of Las Vegas at 1 Yates Rd., 89109. (702) 679-5510. Daily rate including mandatory golf cart: Mon.-Thu. $125; Fri.-Sun. $150. **Lakes course** is 18 holes; 6008 yards; par 71; 69.3 rating; 120 slope; **Desert course** is 18 holes; 6085 yards; par 72; 69.5 rating; 124 slope. Clubhouse, golf shop, professional, power carts, rental clubs, driving range; cocktail lounge.

Spring Mountains National Recreation Area

MOUNT CHARLESTON GOLF RESORT Public
30 miles northwest of Las Vegas on SR 157, near Mount Charleston Hotel; 515 Kyle Canyon Rd., Las Vegas, 89124. (702) 872-4653. Daily rate including mandatory golf cart: $40 for 9 holes, $55 for 18 holes. The course is 9 holes; 3106 yards; par 70 (9 holes twice); N/A rating. Golf shop, professional, power carts, rental clubs, driving range; snack bar.

Horseback Riding
Las Vegas

COWBOY TRAIL RIDES, INC.
1211 S. Eastern Ave., 89124. (702) 387-2457. Open daily. Guided rides ranging from 1 hour to overnight; prices from $25 to $239, depending on length of ride. Reservations recommended. Riders traverse scenic Red Rock Canyon on trips that contain mustang viewing, rim rides, twilight barbecues as well as a combo helicopter ride packages.

Red Rock Canyon National Conservation Area

BONNIE SPRINGS OLD NEVADA
Off SR 159/W. Charleston Blvd., 5½ miles south of Red Rock Canyon Visitor Center; 1 Gun Fighter Ln., 89004. (702) 875-4191. Open daily; first ride departs at 9 a.m., last at 3:15 p.m., Jun. through Sep. at 5:45 p.m. $18 per person. No reservations. One-hour guided rides traverse scenic Red Rock Canyon.

Spring Mountains National Recreation Area

SAGE BRUSH RANCH *Stables: 12000 W. Ann Rd., Las Vegas; mail: 4880 Spanish Wells Dr., North Las Vegas 89030. (702) 645-9422. Open daily. $25-105. Reservations required.* Rides may include breakfast, lunch or dinner and may traverse through Red Rock Canyon.

Rock Climbing
Red Rock Canyon National Conservation Area

SKY'S THE LIMIT *HCR 33 Box 1, 89124. (702) 363-4533, (800) 733-7597. Half-day rock climbing lessons, $169.*

Outdoor activities include horsing around with a new friend at Red Rock Canyon.

Reservations recommended. Participants learn climbing and rappelling fundamentals from experienced instructors amid the scenery of Red Rock Canyon. Climbing shoes and equipment are provided. Day hikes also available.

Tennis & Racquetball

Tennis and racquetball enthusiasts will find plenty of places to hone their skills in Las Vegas. A number of publicly maintained parks have courts, as do many of the resort hotels and private clubs. Most of the courts are lighted for nighttime play. The hotels that allow visitors to use their facilities often give priority to their registered guests, restricting others to open courts. Hotels whose courts are for guests only are not listed here. It is always a good

idea to phone ahead, since hours and regulations governing play are subject to change.

The public courts operate on a first-come, first-served basis and are open daily, generally from 6 a.m. to 11 p.m. For information about public courts, call (702) 455-8245.

Las Vegas

BALLY'S LAS VEGAS Semi-Private
3645 Las Vegas Blvd. S., 89109. (702) 739-4598. Hotel guests, $8 per hour; nonguests, $15 per hour. Reservations required for play between 7 a.m. and 7 p.m. 8 lighted outdoor tennis courts.

DESERT INN Semi-Private
3145 Las Vegas Blvd. S., 89109. (702) 733-4577. 6 a.m.-10 p.m. Hotel guests, free; nonguests, $10 per-person daily pass. Reservations available. 4 lighted tennis courts.

FLAMINGO HILTON-LAS VEGAS Semi-Private
3555 Las Vegas Blvd. S., 89109. (702) 733-3444. $12 per hour for hotel guests, $20 for nonguests. 4 lighted tennis courts.

HIDDEN PALMS PARK Public
8855 Hidden Palms Pkwy., 89123. 2 lighted tennis courts.

LAS VEGAS ATHLETIC CLUB-MARYLAND PARKWAY Semi-Private
2655 S. Maryland Pkwy, 89104. (702) 734-5822. Open 24 hours. Guest pass, $10. Reservations available. 5 racquetball courts.

LAS VEGAS ATHLETIC CLUB-WEST SAHARA Semi-Private
5200 W. Sahara Ave., 89102. (702) 364-5822. Open daily; Mon.-Fri. 5 a.m.-midnight, Sat.-Sun. 7 a.m.-8 p.m. Guest

pass $10. Reservations available. 2 racquetball courts, 25-meter lap pool.

LAS VEGAS SPORTING HOUSE
Semi-Private
3025 Industrial Rd., 89109. (702) 733-8999. Open 24 hours. $15 per person, includes all facilities. 10 racquetball courts; 2 squash courts; 2 lighted tennis courts.

LAURELWOOD PARK Public
4300 Newcastle Rd., 89103. 2 lighted tennis courts.

MGM GRAND HOTEL CASINO
Semi-Private
3799 Las Vegas Blvd. S., 89109. (702) 891-3085. Hotel guests $15, nonguests $20. Reservations advised. 4 lighted tennis courts. Racquet rentals, lessons, ball machine.

MONTE CARLO RESORT & CASINO Semi-Private
3770 Las Vegas Blvd. S., 89109. (702) 730-7411. Hotel guests $10, nonguests

$15. Reservations required. 3 lighted tennis courts.

PARADISE PARK COMMUNITY CENTER Public
4770 S. Harrison Dr., 89121. 2 lighted tennis courts.

PAUL MEYER PARK Public
4525 New Forest Dr., 89117. 2 lighted tennis courts.

SUNRISE PARK AND COMMUNITY CENTER Public
2240 Linn Ln., 89115. 2 lighted tennis courts.

SUNSET PARK TENNIS Private
2601 E. Sunset Rd., 89120. (702) 260-9803. 7 a.m.-7 p.m. $3 per hour; 7 p.m.-11 p.m. $5 per person, per hour. Reservations suggested. 8 lighted tennis courts. Tennis socials and lessons.

UNIVERSITY OF NEVADA, LAS VEGAS Semi-Private
McDermott Complex, on campus near

The desert climate offers nearly ideal playing conditions year round.

Harmon Ave. and Swenson St. Tennis reservations (702) 895-4489; racquetball reservations (702) 895-3150. Tennis courts open daily 8 a.m.-10 p.m. Guest fee $5. Racquetball courts open daily; Mon.-Fri. 6 a.m.-10 p.m., Sat. 8 a.m.-6 p.m., Sun. 10 a.m.-6 p.m. Guest fee, $2. Reservations advised. 12 lighted tennis courts; 8 indoor racquetball courts.

WHITNEY PARK AND COMMU-NITY CENTER Public
5700 E. Missouri Ave., 89122. 3 lighted tennis courts.

WINCHESTER PARK AND COM-MUNITY CENTER Public
3130 S. McLeod Dr., 89121. 2 lighted tennis courts.

WINTERWOOD PARK Public
5310 Consul Ave., 89122. 2 lighted tennis courts.

Laughlin

MOUNTAIN VIEW PARK Public
Needles Hwy., south of Desert Rd. 2 lighted tennis courts.

Water Recreation

Entries for this section are listed north to south in three regions along the Colorado River: Lake Mead, Lake Mohave and Below Davis Dam. The first two fall within the Lake Mead National Recreation Area, which stretches from the upper reaches of Lake Mead to Davis Dam at the southern tip of Lake Mohave. The river below Davis Dam includes the Laughlin/Bullhead City area and southward toward Needles, California.

Lake Mead

25 miles southeast of Las Vegas; 4 miles northeast of Boulder City. Information

available through the Lake Mead National Recreation Area at either the Alan Bible Visitor Center on US 93, phone (702) 293-8990 or (702) 293-8906, or at any park ranger station. Elevation 1200. This 110-mile-long lake on the Colorado River extends from Hoover Dam to the Grand Canyon. The shoreline offers sandy beaches and sheltered coves, while the rugged desert terrain invites hiking and climbing. Lake activities encompass boating, swimming, sailing, water-skiing, scuba diving, sailboarding, use of

▼ *Spa Facilities*

After a long day of exploring the diverse offerings of Las Vegas, your tired and aching muscles may be screaming out for a relaxing massage, facial or an herbal wrap. On the other hand, maybe your body is used to a regular workout and you feel guilty about lounging around the hotel pool or casino all day, or worse, the number of buffets you've been frequenting. Alas, help is on the way! Many of the large resort hotels feature complete spa facilities, including whirlpool, sauna, massage, exercise programs (aquatic, aerobic), gym equipment, and more. Hotel spa and health club privileges often carry a fee; policies vary at each establishment. Some health clubs in hotels admit only registered guests. Public health clubs are numerous in the city, and most of the larger ones offer daily passes; check the local telephone directory yellow pages under "Health Clubs" for further information.

personal watercraft and fishing.
Complete recreation facilities are available at six sites operated by concessionaires of the National Park Service.
Boaters should beware of sudden winds, floating debris, and underwater rocks and shoals caused by fluctuating water levels.

Boating

CALLVILLE BAY RESORT AND MARINA *22 miles northeast of Henderson on SR 167, 4 miles south of Northshore Rd.; Box 100, HCR 30, Las Vegas, NV 89124. (702) 565-8958. Open daily.* Paved launch ramp, temporary mooring, slips, dry storage, auto/boat fuel, engine repairs, marine waste station. Rentals: houseboats, motorboats (15 to 250 h.p.), fishing tackle, jet skis, houseboats. Marine hardware, campground, picnic area.

ECHO BAY RESORT AND MARINA *30 miles south of Overton off Northshore Rd., Overton, NV 89040. (702) 394-4066. Open daily.* Paved launch ramp, temporary mooring, slips, dry storage, auto/boat fuel, engine and hull repairs, marine waste station. Rentals: houseboats, motorboats (15 to 150 h.p.), fishing tackle, water-skis, personal watercraft. Marine hardware, bait, groceries, ice, snack bar, restaurant, lodging, campground, picnic area.

HEMENWAY LAUNCH RAMP *5 miles northeast of Boulder City off Lakeshore Rd.; Lake Mead National Recreation Area, 601 Nevada Hwy., Boulder City, NV 89005. (702) 293-8990. Open daily.* Paved launch ramp. Wheelchair-accessible fishing dock nearby.

Lake Mead National Recreation Area features a variety of water sports.

LAKE MEAD RESORT AND MARINA *7 miles northeast of Boulder City; 322 Lakeshore Rd., Boulder City, NV 89005. (702) 293-3484. Open daily.* Paved launch ramp, slips, temporary mooring, dry storage, boat fuel. Rentals: motorboats (140 h.p.). Lodging, public campgrounds, restaurant, store; picnic area nearby.

LAS VEGAS BAY MARINA *8 miles northeast of Henderson off Lakeshore Rd.; P.O. Box 91150, Henderson, NV 89009. (702) 565-9111. Open daily.* Paved launch ramp, temporary mooring, slips, dry storage, auto/boat fuel, engine and hull repairs, marine waste station. Rentals: motorboats (15 to 185 h.p.), water-skis, waverunners. Marine hardware, bait, groceries, ice, restaurant, campground, picnic area.

OVERTON BEACH RESORT AND MARINA *11 miles southeast of Overton off Lakeshore Rd., Overton, NV 89040. (702) 394-4040. Open daily.*

Closed Dec. 25. Paved launch ramp, temporary mooring, slips, dry storage, auto/boat fuel, engine and hull repairs, marine waste station. Rentals: fishing boat, patio boat, personal watercraft. Marine hardware, bait, groceries, ice, snack bar, RV sites with hookups.

TEMPLE BAR RESORT AND MARINA *28 miles northeast of US 93 at end of Temple Bar Rd.; P.O. Box 545, Temple Bar, AZ 86443. (520) 767-3211. Open daily. Closed Dec. 25.* Paved launch ramp, mooring, slips, dry storage, auto/boat fuel, engine/hull repairs, marine waste station. Rentals: motorboats (15 to 150 h.p.), water-skis, personal watercraft. Cocktail lounge, Marine hardware, bait, groceries, ice, restaurant, lodging, public campground, picnic area.

Fishing

Lake Mead offers some of the country's best fishing. Unlike some lakes, Lake Mead (and nearby Lake Mohave) has an open season on all species of fish year round. Largemouth bass, striped bass, channel catfish, black crappie and bluegill are popular catches; rangers or marina personnel can help point out the best fishing areas. Striped bass are most popular; some have tipped the scales at 50 pounds or more. A wheel-chair-accessible fishing dock is located at Hemenway Fishing Point on Boulder Beach.

Swimming

Clear and clean water ideal for swimming, snorkeling and diving can be found at Lake Mead. The best seasons are spring, summer and fall, when water

▼ *Houseboating*

Houseboats are permitted on Lake Mead, Lake Mohave and on the 75-mile stretch of the Colorado River from Davis Dam south to Parker Dam. There are 246 square miles of uncrowded, open waters for houseboaters on Lake Mead. The numerous secluded coves and scenic steep-walled canyons along its 550 miles of shoreline make the area popular with boaters. The Colorado River section from Davis Dam south offers varied scenery, including rugged mountains, marshes, a narrow canyon (south of Needles) and the wide expanse of Lake Havasu. Lake Mohave has numerous coves and inlets to explore at the south end of the lake, including many sandy coves. The mild winter weather and hot summer days make houseboating popular all year in each of these areas; however, summer thunderstorms are common. Reservations should be made well in advance. Houseboats can be rented at the following locations—Lake Mead: Callville Bay Resort and Marina, (800) 255-5561; Echo Bay Resort, (800) 752-9669. Lake Mohave: Cottonwood Cove Resort and Marina, (800) 255-5561; Lake Mohave Resort, (800) 752-9669.

temperatures average about 78 degrees. Boulder Beach is a designated swimming area. Swim with caution and with a buddy, as no lifeguard services are provided. The scuba diving trail at north Boulder Beach provides a protected dive area.

Water-Skiing

The lake's wide basins offer perfect conditions for water-skiing. The sport is allowed on most of Lake Mead, except in the side canyons and north of Hoover Dam for a few hundred feet.

Lake Mohave

Accessible via US 95 and US 93. Information available through the Lake Mead National Recreation Area at either the Alan Bible Visitor Center (near Lake Mead on US 93), phone (702) 293-8990 or (702) 293-8906, or at any park ranger station. Elevation 675. This narrow lake, which stretches for 67 miles below Hoover Dam to Davis Dam, is lined by rock canyon walls, and has numerous coves and sandy beaches. Activities include boating, swimming, water-skiing, skin diving, sailboarding, use of personal watercraft, and fishing. Boating facilities are located at three points along the lake. Boaters should beware of sudden winds and flash floods.

Boating

COTTONWOOD COVE RESORT AND MARINA *14 miles east of Searchlight at end of Cottonwood Cove Rd.; P.O. Box 1000, Cottonwood Cove, NV 89046. (702) 297-1464. Open daily.* Paved launch ramp, slips, dry storage, auto/boat fuel, engine repairs, temporary mooring, marine waste station. Rentals: Houseboats, motorboats (25 to 150 h.p.), personal watercraft, water-skis. Bait, groceries, ice, clothing, restaurant, lodging, RV sites with hookups, picnic and swimming areas.

LAKE MOHAVE RESORT AND MARINA *At Katherine Landing, 6 miles north of Bullhead City via Arizona SR 68 and Katherine Landing Rd., Bullhead City, AZ, 86430. (520) 754-3245. Open daily.* Paved launch ramp, slips, temporary mooring, dry storage, boat fuel, engine repairs, marine waste station. Rentals: houseboats, motorboats (15 to 150 h.p.), fishing tackle, water-skis, personal watercraft, houseboats. Marine hardware, bait, groceries, ice, snack bar, restaurant, lodging, RV sites with hookups, picnic area. Wheelchair-accessible fishing dock nearby.

PRINCESS COVE LAUNCH RAMP *Follow a graded dirt road 5 miles north of Katherine Landing, Bullhead City. (520) 754-3272.* Paved launch ramp.

▼ *More on the River*

Visitors will find the Auto Club's *Guide to Colorado River* a useful recreation map of the Colorado River. The guide provides detailed map coverage and information on local activities, attractions, events and facilities. Members can obtain this publication at all Auto Club district offices in California and Nevada. Nonmembers should check with a local bookseller in Central or Southern California.

WILLOW BEACH HARBOR

14 miles south of Hoover Dam via US 93 and Willow Beach Rd.; Willow Beach, AZ 86445. (520) 767-4747. Open daily. Closed Dec. 25. Paved launch ramp, slips, boat fuel, marine waste station. Rentals: motorboats (25 to 150 h.p.), personal watercraft. Bait, groceries, ice, picnic area.

Fishing

Noted for its rainbow trout and bass fishing, Lake Mohave offers an open season on all species of fish year round. Trout spend the summer north of Willow Beach and migrate south from October through January; a fish hatchery at Willow Beach provides trout for planting in the lake. Rainbow trout are popular in the cold waters of upper Lake Mohave from Hoover Dam to Willow Beach, but the record sizes of the past have diminished to an occasional five pounds. Large-mouth bass prefer the deep water at the south end of the lake and only move into shallow water to spawn; the best catches are taken from October to May. Trolling live bait at depths of 10 to 30 feet works well to lure them; fishing the coves with floating minnow-shaped lures is also effective during the midday hours. Striped bass have become an increasingly common catch throughout much of the lake in recent years. July and August are the best months for finding catfish in the lake's small coves and inlets. February through April is crappie season; they can be found along the lower half of the lake. Mini-jigs, worms and minnows are the ticket for catching them. A wheelchair-accessible fishing dock is located at Katherine Landing. **Note:** There is a multiagency effort under way to protect endangered species of the Colorado River. Fishermen should identify and immediately release humpback chubs,

bonytail chubs, razorback suckers and Colorado squawfish that they hook. Anglers who are unfamiliar with these species will find descriptions in the California and Arizona fishing regulations booklets that are available where licenses are sold.

Swimming

Lake Mohave offers swimming, snorkeling and diving in clear waters. Except for the northern reaches of the lake, where the water is quite cold, the water averages about 78 degrees during spring, summer and fall.

Water-Skiing

Water-skiing is permitted on all of Lake Mohave except along a 21-mile stretch of the Colorado River extending south from Hoover Dam to Chalk Cliffs.

Colorado River: Below Davis Dam

Accessible via Arizona SR 95. Elevation 550. This stretch of the Colorado River is bordered by mobile home parks and the many casinos of Laughlin, Nevada. Activities include swimming, water-skiing, sailboarding, use of personal watercraft and fishing. Supplies and tourist facilities are available in Bullhead City and Laughlin, and boat launching ramps are scattered along the shoreline.

Boating

BULLHEAD CITY ROTARY PARK *2315 Balboa Dr.; mail: 1255 Marina Blvd., Bullhead City, AZ 86442. (520) 763-9400 ext. 257. Open daily.*

Paved launch ramp ($10 entry fee in summer). Picnic area.

DAVIS CAMP COUNTY PARK
Mohave County Park; P.O. Box 2078, Bullhead City, AZ 86430. (520) 754-4606. Open daily. $3 entry fee. Paved launch ramp, dry storage. Ice, tent and RV sites, picnic area.

LAZY HARRY'S *Off Riverview Dr; 2170 Rio Grande Rd., Bullhead City, AZ 86442. (520) 758-6322. Open daily.* Paved launch ramp. Ice, restaurant, picnic area.

▼ Fishing Licenses

Anglers fishing from Arizona, California and Nevada must possess valid fishing licenses from the state concerned. In Arizona, persons under age 14 do not require a license, while in California persons under age 16 do not require one. In Nevada a junior permit is required for anglers 12 to 15 years old. The rules and regulations of each state must be strictly adhered to, including within the Lake Mead National Recreation Area. Fishing on the Colorado River or Lake Mead requires a "special use" stamp affixed to a state fishing license. An additional stamp is required for trout fishing. Fishing from shore on an Indian Reservation requires a special fishing permit. Licenses and further information are available from the marinas or at local bait and tackle shops.

Fishing

Rainbow trout are the most popular catch along this stretch of the river; they inhabit the cold water along the gravel beds below Davis Dam (no fishing in posted areas). Trout are also planted south of Laughlin-Bullhead City near the California-Nevada state line from October to June. During warm weather, the fish are attracted to lures such as Super Dupers, Panther Martins, and spinners and spoons. (No, we're not making this up.) In cooler weather, the best bet is live bait, mostly night crawlers and marshmallow combos. The fish stay in deep water during the day and move toward shore at night.

Anglers can also fill their creels with good-sized catfish, largemouth bass, and plenty of bluegill and crappie. Bass prefer the cooler deep water and will hit on live bait or floating lures. Catfish like stink baits (garlic cheese), dough balls, anchovies and night crawlers. Bluegill and crappie hit on almost anything that moves—try worms for bluegill, and minnows or mini-jigs for crappie.

Striped bass are a popular game fish, and they often tip the scales at around 30 pounds. The largest striper ever caught in an inland habitat was landed at Bullhead City and weighed in at 59 pounds, 12 ounces. These fish winter at Lake Havasu and start moving north in the spring, hitting the Laughlin-Bullhead City area in May; common baits are shad, frozen anchovies or sardines, with sinkers to keep the bait below the surface of the water. The Striper Derby is traditionally held from Memorial Day through Labor Day. Call the Bullhead Area Chamber of Commerce at (520) 754-4121 for the current status of the event.

The beach at Harrah's Laughlin is a pleasant spot for taking a dip and enjoying the sight of passing riverboats.

LAUGHLIN SPORTFISHING

Harrah's Casino Hotel boat dock, 2900 W. Casino Dr., Laughlin; P.O. Box 29010, 89029. (702) 298-6828. Open daily, weather permitting; boat departs at 6 a.m. $75 per person. Reservations required. Half-day boat excursions on the Colorado River provide fishing opportunities for trout and striped bass. All bait and tackle supplied.

Inner Tubing

Inner tubing is a popular sport along the Colorado River. For easy pickup and parking, swimmers usually launch their inner tubes from Davis Camp County Park, north of Bullhead City, Arizona, and float four or five miles south along the river, disembarking at Bullhead Community Park.

Swimming

Swimming in the river should not be attempted except from designated beach areas. A public beach is located at Davis Camp County Park on the Arizona side of the river (north of Bullhead City on SR 95). The best swimming in the area is at Lake Mohave. In the summer the lake water can get as warm as 80 degrees. **Note: A word of caution to river swimmers south of Davis Dam—the water released from the dam is very cold, about 60 degrees.**

Water-Skiing

Water-skiing is allowed along the Colorado River from Bullhead City south to Needles. A sparsely populated area just south of Bullhead City is usually the best choice for the sport.

Transportation

*A rich variety of transportation choices to **Las Vegas** and **Laughlin** make getting there easy for conventioneers, families and groups of singles. Both desert cities boast international airports, convenient bus service and well-maintained roads.*

Air

For complete schedule information and help arranging flights from cities with direct or connecting service, contact any **Auto Club Travel Agency** office, or phone the Auto Club's Airline Express Desk. In Southern California call (800) 222-5000, Monday through Friday from 8 a.m. to 6 p.m.

LAUGHLIN/BULLHEAD INTERNATIONAL AIRPORT *600 Hwy. 95, Bullhead City, AZ 86429. (520) 754-2134.* This $23 million airport is located in Arizona just minutes from the casino gaming action across the river. The 7500-foot-by-150-foot runway accommodates aircraft as large as DC-10s, and is served by two commuter airlines and three charter carriers. About 100 flights are logged each week, serving more than 230,000 passengers a year. Taxis and free hotel shuttles serve the airport, and several car rental agencies have offices here.

McCarran International Airport serves more than 30 million passengers annually.

McCARRAN INTERNATIONAL AIRPORT *1 mile from the Las Vegas Strip; 5757 Wayne Newton Blvd., Las Vegas 89119. (702) 261-5211; TDD (702) 261-3111.* McCarran is the 10th busiest airport in the U.S. and 18th busiest in the world, with more than 30 million passengers passing through it each year. More than 40 air carriers serve Las Vegas, among them 23 scheduled airlines, two commuter lines and up to 20 charter airlines (depending on the season). The airport also provides international service to Belgium, Canada, Germany, Japan and seasonal flights to the United Kingdom.

As Las Vegas's tourism industry grows, so must the ancillary structures that support tourism. The airport, for example, has experienced a 60 percent increase in passenger traffic since 1990. In order to accommodate this increase as well as to provide room for future anticipated growth, a use plan has been developed for McCarran International Airport that will guide it well into the 21st century. The most recent expansion was the opening of the new D Gates. These additional gates will allow McCarran to serve 45 million passengers annually. It should be noted that all ticketing and baggage functions still occur in Terminal 1.

Private shuttle buses, taxis, limousines and public buses make pickups at McCarran. The Citizens Area Transit (CAT) number "108" and "109" buses serve the airport; call (702) 228-7433 for further details. Ground transportation services at McCarran are abundant, see

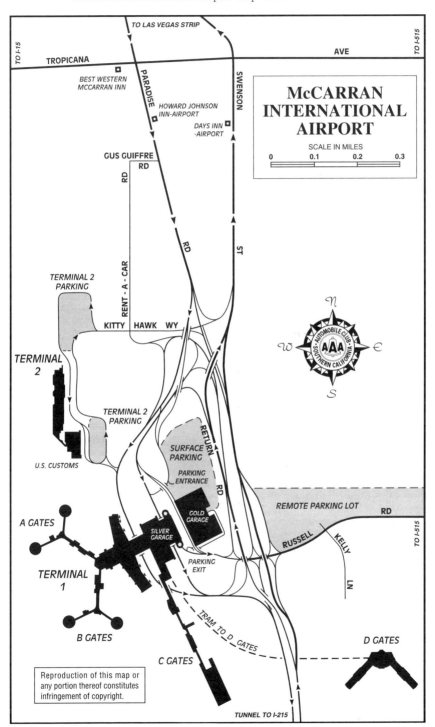

TO LAS VEGAS STRIP

TO I-15

TO I-515

TROPICANA   AVE

PARADISE

SWENSON

BEST WESTERN
McCARRAN INN

HOWARD JOHNSON
INN-AIRPORT

DAYS INN
-AIRPORT

McCARRAN INTERNATIONAL AIRPORT

SCALE IN MILES

0   0.1   0.2   0.3

GUS GUIFFRE
RD

RD

RD

ST

TERMINAL 2
PARKING

RENT - A - CAR

N

W   E

S

AUTOMOBILE CLUB · SOUTHERN CALIFORNIA
AAA

KITTY   HAWK   WY

TERMINAL
2

TERMINAL 2
PARKING

RETURN

SURFACE
PARKING

PARKING
ENTRANCE

RD

U.S. CUSTOMS

REMOTE PARKING LOT   RD

GOLD
GARAGE

A GATES

SILVER
GARAGE

TO I-515

RUSSELL

KELLY

TERMINAL
1

PARKING
EXIT

LN

B GATES

TRAM TO D GATES

D GATES

C GATES

TUNNEL TO I-215

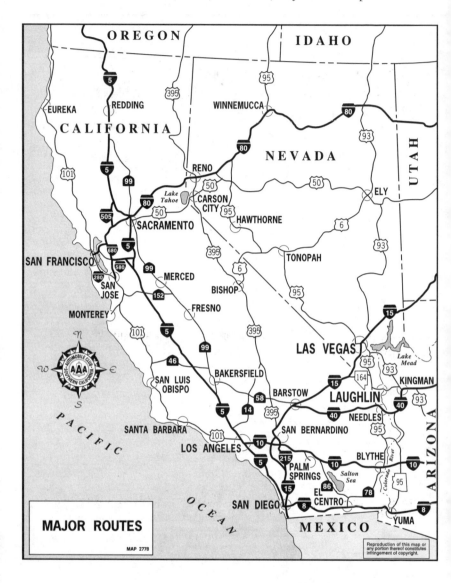

MAJOR ROUTES

MAP 2778

Reproduction of this map or any portion thereof constitutes infringement of copyright.

the Las Vegas telephone directory yellow pages under "Airport Transportation & Parking Services." All major car rental companies have offices at McCarran; refer to the yellow pages under "Automobile Renting and Leasing." The Auto Club's Travel Agency offices and Airline Express Desk can also help arrange reservations for a car rental.

Automobile

Las Vegas entertains millions of visitors each year, and not surprisingly more than half of them arrive by automobile. More than 4 million people a year drive to Nevada's largest city from the state of California. Southern Californians account for most of the automobile

▼ *Desert Driving Hints*

Regardless of the point of departure, any automobile trip from California to Las Vegas will involve some desert driving. At all times, but especially during the summer months, some basic precautions should be taken when planning to cross the Mojave Desert.

- Check the condition of your car's engine and cooling systems and make sure they're in good working order. Look closely for radiator leaks, worn fan belts and cracked hoses.

- Take about five gallons of water in a clean container for emergency purposes—both for the car's radiator and for drinking. If your car overheats, do not remove the radiator cap immediately because of the risk of explosion. After the engine has cooled, slowly remove the cap and add water, leaving about an inch of air space between the water level and the top of the radiator. If an older model car experiences vapor lock, wrap a wet towel around the gas line between the fuel pump and the carburetor. Caution should be used in order to insure that the towel does not become entangled in any moving parts (belts). This may cool the line and allow the car to start.

- Make certain that your car's tires are properly inflated before starting out. If the tires become overly hard while crossing the desert, do not release any air. Instead, stop the car and allow the tires to cool, then proceed. Before setting out, inspect the spare tire and inflate to proper pressure.

- Watch the gasoline gauge and buy fuel when it is available. Towns in the Mojave Desert are few and far between; don't get stuck without gas and no place to get it.

- If your car becomes disabled, activate the hazard warning lights once safely out of the traffic lane and raise your hood. Do not abandon the car to go for help. Not only is it often a long walk to the nearest town or telephone, but extreme desert temperatures in the summer months bring a real threat of heat stroke—even a short walk could become dangerous.

Note: Desert driving often means that travelers must take "out of the ordinary" precautions in an emergency. For instance, pulling your car as far off the road as possible in an emergency is usually the most desirable action to take. Many areas of desert terrain do not offer a firm gravel surface off the asphalt shoulder, however, so be aware that driving onto a shoulder of soft sand may mean a tow truck will be required to get your car back onto the road.

When weather permits, motorists should follow normal emergency procedures: remain in your car, in the seat that is the farthest from moving traffic, keep the seat belt fastened and headrest properly positioned, keep doors locked and wait for assistance. In extreme desert heat these procedures will not be possible—even with the windows rolled down, the car will become unbearably hot. In such cases, seek out a shady area to wait for highway assistance, either in the shadow of the vehicle itself or in the shade of nearby vegetation. Do not leave pets or children in the car—they suffer the effects of the heat even more quickly than adults.

When faced with a disabled car, the best course of action the Auto Club can recommend is to wait for Highway Patrol assistance. Emergency call boxes are numerous along well-traveled highways, and cellular phones can be convenient tools for getting swift assistance. Highway Patrol officers also routinely make regular patrols of desert highways. Motorists should use extreme caution in accepting help from strangers.

traffic. With the 70 mph speed limit in effect on I-15, Las Vegs is only about a 5½-hour drive from Los Angeles; from San Diego it is about an hour farther. The San Francisco Bay Area is some 11 hours away by car, exclusive of stops. Although the 70 mph speed limit is in effect for almost all of the driving along I-15 in both California and Nevada, weather and road conditions often dictate a lower speed. For current highway conditions, call the Nevada Department of Transportation at (702) 486-3116 (recording); in California call (800) 927-7623. Drivers should also be alert to lower posted speed limits in populated areas.

Laughlin is approximately the same distance from Los Angeles as is Las Vegas. The routes from Los Angeles to both Las Vegas and Laughlin begin in a similar manner: I-10 east past Ontario, then north on I-15 to Barstow. At Barstow those bound for Las Vegas continue on I-15. For Laughlin, motorists take I-40 east across the Mojave Desert toward Needles. Near Needles there are two possible routes for the remainder of the drive to Laughlin: about 10 miles west of Needles motorists can take US 95 north 24 miles, then take SR 163 east 18 miles to Laughlin Civic Drive; or about four miles west of Needles, there's an alternate route along Needles Highway (River Road) north to Laughlin. To get to the Arizona side of the river, SR 95 and Bullhead City, there's now a choice of three bridges (listed south to north): Needles, Veterans and Laughlin.

For **emergency roadside assistance**, AAA members may call **(800) AAA-HELP** in the USA and Canada; **(800) 955-4TDD** for the hearing impaired.

Bus

Greyhound/Trailways offers service to Las Vegas from virtually any town in California and Nevada. Reservations are not accepted, and tickets can usually be purchased just prior to departure. In Las Vegas, Greyhound/Trailways uses the downtown bus terminal building at 200 South Main Street (at Carson Avenue); phone (800) 231-2222.

The route for bus travelers to Laughlin-Bullhead City is through Needles, California, or Las Vegas, Nevada. From there, both Greyhound/Trailways and K-T Services bus lines provide daily service to Laughlin; the trip takes about 2½ hours. Don Laughlin's Riverside Resort Hotel & Casino, South Tower, is the terminus in Laughlin for both bus lines. Both companies also serve Bullhead City, with pickups and drop-offs at the River Queen Motel, 125 Long Street. For more information, phone Greyhound/Trailways at (702) 298-1934 or (800) 231-2222, or K-T Services at (702) 644-2233.

Train

While many Southern Californians would like to take Amtrak to and from Las Vegas, as of press time there was no train service available for travel between these two cities, although plans are in development for train service at some future time. Amtrak currently offers service utilizing buses. Traveling time from Los Angeles to Las Vegas is 5½ hours. For fare and schedule information, call Amtrak at (800) 872-7245. For reservations and help in arranging connecting trains or buses, contact any Travel Agency office of the Automobile Club of Southern California.

Tourist Information Sources

*The chambers of commerce and visitor information bureaus listed below are resources for obtaining additional information about **Las Vegas, Laughlin** and surrounding areas. AAA/CSAA district offices provide travel services and publications, and highway information to Auto Club members.*

Chambers of Commerce & Visitor Information Bureaus

Boulder City Chamber of Commerce
1305 Arizona St.
Boulder City, NV 89005
(702) 293-2034
Office hours: Mon.-Fri. 9 a.m.-5 p.m.

Bullhead Area Chamber of Commerce
1251 Hwy. 95
Bullhead City, AZ 86429
(520) 754-4121
Office hours: Mon.-Fri. 9 a.m.-5 p.m., Sat. 10 a.m.-2 p.m.

Las Vegas Convention and Visitors Authority
3150 Paradise Rd.
Las Vegas, NV 89109
(702) 892-7575, 892-0711
Office hours: Mon.-Fri. 8 a.m.-6 p.m., Sat.-Sun. 8 a.m.-5 p.m.

Laughlin Visitors Bureau
1555 S. Casino Dr.
P.O. Box 502
Laughlin, NV 89029
(702) 298-3321
Office hours: Daily 8 a.m.-5 p.m.

Nevada Welcome Center
100 Nevada Hwy.
Boulder City, NV 89005
Office hours: Daily 8:30 a.m.-4:30 p.m.

Auto Club District Offices

Automobile Club of Southern California district offices can help members in preparing a trip to anywhere in the world. For travel within the United States, Canada and Mexico, the Club can make reservations for lodging and transportation, and provide weather, routing and emergency road service information. The Auto Club's Travel Agency can make airline, train and package tour reservations for travel throughout the world.

Auto Club members can also take advantage of discounts on lodging, as indicated in the AAA *California/Nevada TourBook*, available free to members. The Auto Club's *Member Saver* is published monthly and is a valuable source for seasonal discounts on events and points of interest.

The following AAA/California State Automobile Association district offices are located in the Las Vegas region.

Henderson
601-A Whitney Ranch Rd.
Henderson, NV 89014
(702) 458-2323
Office hours: Mon.-Fri. 8:30 a.m.-5:30 p.m.

Las Vegas
3312 W. Charleston Blvd.
Las Vegas, NV 89102
(702) 870-9171
Office hours: Mon.-Fri. 8:30 a.m.-5:30 p.m.

Summerlin
8440 W. Lake Mead, Ste. 203
Las Vegas, NV 89128
(702) 360-3151
Office hours: Mon.-Fri. 8:30 a.m.-5:30 p.m.

Lodging & Restaurants

*Despite the fact that **Las Vegas** has more than 100,000 rooms available, it is important to make reservations as far in advance as possible. "No vacancy" signs are constant reminders that the town operates at near capacity all year. During peak periods, a one-night reservation for Friday or Saturday night is difficult to obtain.*

There are several things to be considered in addition to price when staying in Las Vegas. It is easier to obtain reservations to sellout celebrity shows when staying at the hotel where the performer is appearing. If convenient parking is important, a motel would probably be preferable to a hotel. Golf privileges, tennis and spa facilities may also be a consideration.

*__Laughlin__ draws more than 50,000 visitors to its casinos on an average weekend, and holiday crowds can be even larger. While space is limited in Laughlin, additional lodging can also be found across the river in **Bullhead City, Arizona** (listings follow Nevada cities). Passenger ferries provide frequent service from parking lots on the Arizona side of the river to the various casinos on the Nevada side, and 24-hour shuttle bus service is available between the two cities.*

*Lodgings and restaurants are listed alphabetically by city and also include the communities of **Boulder City**, **Cottonwood Cove**, **Echo Bay-Lake Mead**, **Henderson** and **Primm**.*

*T*he properties listed in these pages have been inspected at least once in the past year by a trained representative of AAA. In surprise inspections, each property was found to meet AAA's extensive and detailed requirements for approval. These requirements are reflective of current industry standards and the expectations of the traveling public. Properties are listed alphabetically under the nearest town, with lodging facilities first and restaurants second. Each facility's location is given from the center of town or from the nearest major highway.

Virtually all listings include AAA's "diamond" rating, reflecting the overall quality of the establishment. Many factors are considered in the process of determining the diamond rating. In lodging properties, the facility is first "classified" according to its physical design—is it a motel, a hotel, a resort, an apartment, etc. Since the various types of lodging establishments offer differing amenities and facilities, rating criteria are specific for each classifica-

tion. For example, a motel, which typically offers a room with convenient parking and little if any recreational or public facilities, is rated using criteria designed only for motel-type establishments—it is not compared to a hotel with its extensive public and meeting areas, or to a resort with its wide range of recreational facilities and programs. The diamonds do, however, represent standard levels of quality in all types of establishments.

There is no charge for a property to be listed in AAA publications. However, many lodgings and restaurants have expressed a special desire to attract the AAA member's business. In order to communicate this interest to the traveling public, these facilities have purchased the right to display the ⓐⓐⓐ emblem. As a service to our members, these listings may include more information.

Nearly all lodging and restaurant facilities accept credit cards as forms of payment for services rendered. The following symbols are used to identify the specific cards accepted by each property: AE=American Express, CB=Carte Blanche, DI=Diners Club, DS=Discover, JC=Japanese Credit Bureau, MC=MasterCard, VI=VISA.

Listings which denote "laundry" may offer a coin laundry, valet laundry and/or dry cleaning service. The term "business services" indicates that any of these services are available: personal computers, secretarial services, meeting rooms and conference facilities. Call the establishment to determine if the services and/or facilities you require are offered.

Some lodgings and restaurants listed in Auto Club publications have symbols indicating that they are accessible to individuals with disabilities. The criteria used in qualifying these listings are consistent with, but do not represent the full scope of, the Americans with Disabilities Act of 1990 Accessibility Guidelines (ADAAG). AAA does not evaluate recreational facilities, banquet rooms or convention and meeting facilities for accessibility. Individuals with disabilities are urged to phone ahead to fully understand an establishment's accessibility options.

In accommodations, a ♿ indicates that at least one fully accessible guest room exists and that an individual with mobility impairments will be able to park and enter the building, register, and use at least one food and beverage outlet. For restaurants, the symbol indicates that parking, dining rooms and restrooms are accessible.

The ☷ in a lodging listing means that the following elements are provided: closed-captioned decoders; text telephones; visual notification for fire alarms, incoming phone calls and door knocks; and phone amplification devices.

Lodging

The following accommodations classifications appear in this book.

Apartment—Usually four or more stories with at least half the units equipped for housekeeping. Often in a vacation destination area. Units typically provide a full kitchen, living room and one or more bedrooms, but may be studio-type rooms with kitchen equipment in an alcove. May require a minimum stay and/or offer discounts for longer stays. This classification may also modify any of the other lodging types.

Complex—A combination of two or more kinds of lodgings.

Condominium—A destination property located in a resort area. Guest units consist of a bedroom, living room and kitchen. Kitchens are separate from bedrooms and are equipped with a stove, oven or microwave, refrigerator, cooking utensils and table settings for the maximum number of people occupying the unit. Linens and maid service are provided at least twice weekly. This classification may also modify any of the other lodging types.

Hotel—A multistory building usually including a coffee shop, dining room, lounge, room service, convenience shops, valet, laundry and full banquet/meeting facilities. Parking may be limited.

Motel—Usually one or two stories; food service, if any, consists of a limited facility or snack bar. Often has a pool or playground. Ample parking, usually adjacent to the guest room.

Motor Inn—Usually two or three stories, but may be a high-rise. Generally has recreation facilities, food service and ample parking. May have limited banquet/meeting facilities.

Resort—May be a destination in itself. Has a vacation atmosphere offering extensive recreational facilities for such specific interests as golf, tennis, fishing, etc. Rates may include meals under American or Modified American plans. This classification may also modify any of the other lodging types.

Suite—Units have one or more bedrooms and a living room, which may or may not be closed off from the bedrooms. This classification modifies other lodging types.

A property's diamond rating is not based on the room rate or any one specific aspect of its facilities or operations. Many factors are considered in calculating the rating, and certain minimum standards must be met in all inspection categories. If a property fails approval in just one category, it is not listed in Auto Club publications. The inspection categories include housekeeping, maintenance, service, furnishings and decor. Guest comments received by AAA may also be reviewed in a property's approval/rating process.

These criteria apply to all properties listed in this publication:

• Clean and well-maintained facilities
• Hospitable staff
• Adequate parking
• A well-kept appearance
• Good quality bedding and comfortable beds with adequate illumination
• Good locks on all doors and windows
• Comfortable furnishings and decor
• Smoke detectors
• Adequate towels and supplies
• At least one comfortable easy chair with adequate illumination
• A desk or other writing surface with adequate illumination

Lodging ratings range from one to five diamonds and are defined below:

♦—Good but unpretentious. Establishments are functional. Clean and comfortable rooms must meet the basic needs of privacy and cleanliness.

♦♦—Shows noticeable enhancements in decor and/or quality of furnishings over those at the one-diamond level. May be recently constructed or an older property. Targets the needs of a budget-oriented traveler.

♦♦♦—Offers a degree of sophistication with additional amenities, services and facilities. There is a marked upgrade in services and comfort.

♦♦♦♦—Excellent properties displaying high levels of service and hospitality and offering a wide variety of amenities and upscale facilities, inside the room, on the grounds and in the common areas.

♦♦♦♦♦—Renowned for an exceptionally high degree of service, attractive and luxurious facilities, and many extra amenities. Guest services are executed and presented in a flawless manner. Guests are pampered by a very professional, attentive staff. The property's facilities and operations set standards in hospitality and service.

The diamond ratings shown in this publication are based on inspections done in 1997-98. Occasionally a property is listed without a rating, such as when an establishment was under construction or undergoing renovations at press time and a rating could not be determined.

Room rates shown in the listings are provided by each establishment's management for publication by AAA. **All rates are subject to change.** During special events or holiday periods, rates may exceed those published, and special discounts or savings programs may not be honored. High-season rates are always shown; off-season rates are listed if they are substantially lower than the rest of the year. Rates are for typical rooms, not special units, and do not include taxes.

Many properties make special and discounted rates available exclusively to AAA members. Two publications list these rates: the AAA *TourBook*, which is published annually, and the Auto Club's *Member Saver*, a monthly newsletter featuring short-term rates and packages that offer discounts for reservations made through the Auto Club. Both publications are available to AAA members at no charge through Auto Club offices.

Some properties offer discounts to senior citizens, or special rate periods such as weekly or monthly rentals. Inquiries as to the availability of any special discounts should be made at the time of registration. Typically, a property will allow a guest to take advantage of only one discount during his or her stay (i.e., a guest staying at a property offering both a AAA discount and a senior discount may choose only one of the two savings plans).

Each rate line gives the dates for which the rates are valid, the rates for one person (abbreviated 1P), two persons with one bed (2P/1B), two persons with two beds (2P/2B), and the rate for each extra person (XP) not included in the family rate. Figures following these abbreviations are the price(s) for the specified room and occupants. Most rates listed are European plan, which means that no meals are included in the rate. Some lodgings' rates include breakfast [BP] or continental breakfast [CP]. A few properties offer an American Plan [AP], which includes

three meals, or a Modified American Plan [MAP], which offers two meals, usually breakfast and dinner.

Since nearly all establishments have air conditioning, telephones and color cable TV, only the absence of any of these items is noted in the listing. Other facilities, amenities and services, such as movies, massage, in-room whirlpool, child care, massage and recreational activities may have extra fees associated with them. It is best to inquire about these fees when making reservations. Check-in time is shown only if it is after 3 p.m.; check-out time is shown only if it is before 10 a.m. Service charges are not shown unless they are $1 or more, or at least 5 percent of the room rate. If the pet acceptance policy varies within the establishment, no mention of pets is made; it is best to call ahead to verify specifics. By U.S. law, pet restrictions do not apply to guide dogs. Outdoor pools may or may not be heated, and may not be open in winter.

Reservations are always advisable in resort areas and may be the only way to assure obtaining the type of accommodations desired. Deposits are almost always required. Should plans change and reservations need to be canceled, be aware of the amount of notice required to receive a deposit refund.

Many properties welcome children in the same room with their parents at no additional charge; individual listings indicate if there is an age limit. There may be charges for additional equipment, such as roll-aways or cribs. Some properties offer a discount for guests ages 60 and over—be aware that the senior discount cannot usually be taken in conjunction with or in addition to other discounts. Many establishments have a minimum age requirement for renting rooms; in most cases the minimum age is 18, but at some properties the minimum age is 21.

In order to be listed, facilities must have smoke detectors and may have additional fire safety equipment. Listings do not include reference to these items. Members should call the facility in order to obtain more detailed fire-safety information. Many properties have reserved rooms for nonsmokers; look for the ⊘ symbol in the listing. If a smoke-free room is desired, be sure to indicate that request when making a reservation and upon registration.

Restaurants

Restaurants listed in this publication have been found to be consistently good dining establishments. In metropolitan areas, where many restaurants are above average, some of those known for the superiority of their food, service and atmosphere are selected, as well as those offering a selection of quality food at moderate prices (including some cafeterias and family restaurants). In smaller communities, the restaurants considered to be the best in the area may be listed.

The type of cuisine featured at a dining establishment is used as a means of classification for restaurants. There are listings for Steakhouses and Continental cuisine as well as a range of ethnic foods, such as Chinese, Japanese, Italian and yes, American. Special menu types, such as early bird, a la carte, children's or Sunday brunch, are also listed. In many cases something is indicated about each restaurant's atmosphere and appropriate attire. The availability of alcoholic beverages is shown, as well as entertainment and dancing.

Price ranges are for an average, complete meal without alcoholic beverage. Taxes and tips are not included.

▼ Dining Out

Dining in **Las Vegas** is as varied as accommodations. Prices range from as little as $1 for breakfast to more than $50 for gourmet dinners. All of the large hotels have several places to eat, and many have themed dining rooms that feature regional or ethnic decor and food. Many coffee shops are open 24 hours. Buffets are available at almost every major hotel and offer diners a choice of three or four entrees, plus potatoes, vegetables, salads, desserts and a beverage for one price; buffet-style champagne brunches are offered at numerous hotels on weekends.

Similar to Las Vegas, all the large casino/hotels in **Laughlin** have several restaurants, some with themed dining rooms overlooking the river, that feature regional or ethnic foods. Also, a number of restaurants and major fast-food franchise outlets can be found across the river in Bullhead City. Prices in Laughlin range from a low of about $2 for breakfast to a high of $30 for a gourmet dinner. Buffets are common and range in price from $5 to $7, with buffet breakfasts are priced from $2 to $3.50 and lunches priced similarly.

Restaurant ratings are applied to two categories of operational style—full-service eating establishments and self-service, family dining operations such as cafeterias or buffets.

♦—Good but unpretentious dishes. Table settings are usually simple and may include paper place mats and napkins. Alcoholic beverage service, if any, may be limited to beer and wine. Usually informal with an atmosphere conducive to family dining.

♦♦—More extensive menus representing more complex food preparation and, usually, a wider variety of alcoholic beverages. The atmosphere is appealing and suitable for either family or adult dining. Service may be casual, but host or hostess seating can be expected. Table settings may include tablecloths and cloth napkins.

♦♦♦—Extensive or specialized menus and more complex cuisine preparation requiring that a professional chef contribute to either a formal dining experience or a special family meal. Cloth table linens, above-average quality table settings, a skilled service staff and an inviting decor should all be provided. Generally, the wine list includes representatives of the best domestic and foreign wine-producing regions.

♦♦♦♦—An appealing ambiance is often enhanced by fresh flowers and fine furnishings. The overall sophistication and formal atmosphere visually create a dining experience more for adults than for families. A wine steward presents an extensive list of the best wines. A smartly attired, highly skilled staff is capable of describing how any dish is prepared. Elegant silverware, china and correct glassware are typical. The menu includes creative dishes prepared from fresh ingredients by a chef who frequently has international training. Eye-appealing desserts are offered at tableside.

♦♦♦♦♦—A world-class operation with even more luxury and sophistication than four-diamond restaurants. A proportionally large staff, expert in preparing tableside delicacies, provides flawless service. Tables are set with impeccable linens, silver and crystal glassware.

Boulder City

Lodging

BEST WESTERN LIGHTHOUSE INN ⏣

(702) 293-6444; FAX (702) 293-6547.

♦♦ Motel

1 mi E via SR 93; 110 Ville Dr, 89005.

Fri-Sat [CP]	1P $68-85	2P/1B $68-85	2P/2B $68-85
Sun-Thu [CP]	1P $58-75	2P/1B $58-75	2P/2B $58-75

XP $10. Deposit required. AE, CB, DI, DS, MC, VI. Some rooms with view of Lake Mead. 3 stories; exterior corridors. No elevator. **Rooms:** 70. Movies, coffeemakers, refrigerators, ⊘. **Recreation:** Pool, whirlpool. **Services:** Laundry.

EL RANCHO BOULDER MOTEL ⏣

(702) 293-1085; FAX (702) 293-3021.

♦♦ Motel

On US 93 at 725 Nevada Hwy, 89005.

All year	1P $55-70	2P/1B $60-70	2P/2B $60-100

XP $10-20. Deposit required; 17-day refund notice. AE, CB, DI, DS, MC, VI. Spanish-style. Attractive landscaped grounds. 2 stories; exterior corridors. **Rooms:** 39; 7 2-bedroom units. Movies, radios, refrigerators, ⊘. **Recreation:** Pool, whirlpool. **Dining:** Coffee shop nearby.

SANDS MOTEL ⏣

(702) 293-2589; FAX (702) 294-0160.

♦ Motel

On US 93 at 809 Nevada Hwy, 89005.

All year	1P $37-42	2P/1B $42-47	2P/2B $47-52

XP $6; ages 12 and under stay free. Deposit required; 3-day refund notice. AE, CB, DI, DS, MC, VI. 1 story; exterior corridors. **Rooms:** 25; some small units; 2 2-bedroom units. Combination/shower baths, movies, refrigerators, ⊘.

SUPER 8 MOTEL ♦ Motel
(702) 294-8888; FAX (702) 293-4344.
On US 93 at 704 Nevada Hwy, 89005.

Fri-Sat [CP]	1P $56-80	2P/1B $56-80	2P/2B $56-80
Sun-Thu [CP]	1P $44-50	2P/1B $44-50	2P/2B $44-50

XP $5. Deposit required. AE, CB, DI, DS, MC, VI. Pets. 3 stories; exterior corridors. **Rooms:** 114. Movies, radio, ⊘. **Recreation:** Pool. **Services:** Laundry. **Dining:** Nearby dining, cocktail lounge.

Cottonwood Cove
Lodging

COTTONWOOD COVE MOTEL 〔AAA〕 ♦♦ Motel
(702) 297-1464; FAX (702) 297-1464.
Between Las Vegas and Needles; 14 mi E of Searchlight off US 95 at 1000 Cottonwood Cove Rd;
Box 1000, 89046.

2/1-3/31	1P $35	2P/1B $35	2P/2B $35
4/1-5/27	1P $55-60	2P/1B $60	2P/2B $55
5/28-10/31	1P $90-95	2P/1B $95	2P/2B $90

XP $8; ages 5 and under stay free. Deposit required; 14-day refund notice. AE, DS, MC, VI. Gift shop. Gas station and general store. Overlooking Lake Mohave. Beach. 1 story; exterior corridors, **Rooms:** 24. Combination/shower baths. **Recreation:** Swimming, water-skiing, marina, boat ramp, houseboats, power boats and equipment, fishing. **Services:** Laundry. **Dining:** Coffee shop; 8 am-6 pm, 11/1-4/1 from 7 am; $5-14.

Echo Bay-Lake Mead
Lodging

ECHO BAY RESORT 〔AAA〕 ♦♦ Motor Inn
(702) 394-4000; FAX (702) 394-4180.
On Lake Mead, 4 mi E of SR 167; Overton, 89040.

4/1-10/30	1P $69-74	2P/1B $74	2P/2B $69
11/1-3/31	1P $45	2P/1B $45	2P/2B $45

XP $6; age 5 and under stay free. Deposit required; 3-day refund notice. DS, MC, VI. Gift shop. Pets, $5 plus $25 deposit. 2 stories; interior corridors. **Rooms:** 52; 4 family rooms, $84 for up to 4 persons. Lake views, patios or balconies, movies, radios, ⊘; no cable TV. **Recreation:** Fishing, swimming, water-skiing, marina, houseboats, rental boats. **Services:** Laundry, business services. **Dining:** Restaurant, 7 am-8:30 pm; 5/1-9/30, 6 am-9:30 pm; $8-17; cocktail lounge.

Henderson
Lodging

BEST WESTERN LAKE MEAD MOTEL 〔AAA〕 ♦♦ Motel
(702) 564-1712; FAX (702) 564-7642.
Exit US 93/95 at Lake Mead Dr, ½ mi E on SR 146; 85 W Lake Mead Dr, 89015.

5/15-10/15[CP]	1P $56-61	2P/1B $61	2P/2B $61
10/16-5/14 [CP]	1P $51-56	2P/1B $56	2P/2B $56

XP $5; ages 12 and under stay free. Deposit required. Senior discount. AE, CB, DI, DS, MC, VI. 2 stories; exterior corridors. **Rooms:** 59. Movies, refrigerators, ⊘. **Recreation:** Pool. **Services:** Laundry.

THE RESERVE HOTEL CASINO ♦♦♦ Hotel
(702) 558-7000; FAX (702) 567-7373.
Exit US 93/95 at Lake Mead Dr, 777 Lake Mead Dr, 89015.

Fri-Sat	1P $69	2P/1B $69	2P/2B $69
Sun-Thu	1P $49	2P/1B $49	2P/2B $49

Deposit required. AE, CB, DI, DS, MC, VI. Gift shop. 9 stories; interior corridors. Roll-in showers, ▣. **Rooms:** 224. Combination/shower baths, movies, radios, data ports, coffeemakers, refrigerators, ⊘. **Recreation:** Pool. **Services:** Valet parking, laundry. **Dining:** Restaurant.

SUNSET STATION HOTEL & CASINO ⏣ ♦♦♦ Hotel
(702) 547-7744; FAX (702) 547-7744.
From I-15 at I-215 exit to Warm Springs, 7 mi E to Stephanie at 1301 W Sunset Rd, 89104.

Fri-Sat	1P $69-159	2P/1B $69-159	2P/2B $69-159
Sun-Thu	1P $49-139	2P/1B $49-139	2P/2B $49-139

Deposit required. AE, DI, DS, MC, VI. Gift shop. 21 stories; interior corridors. Roll-in showers. **Rooms:** 448. Combination/shower baths, movies, radios, data ports, safes, coffeemakers, refrigerators, ⊘. **Recreation:** Pool, exercise room. **Services:** Valet parking, laundry, airport/area transportation, business services. **Dining:** Restaurant; cocktail lounge; entertainment; night club.

Las Vegas

Lodging

ALEXIS PARK RESORT HOTEL ♦♦♦ Resort Hotel
(702) 796-3300; FAX (702) 796-4334.
I-15 exit E Tropicana Av, 2 blocks W of UNLV, 2 mi S of Convention Center; 375 E Harmon Av, 89109.

4/1-5/31 & 9/1-9/30	1P $135-375	2P/1B $135-375	2P/2B $135-375
6/1-8/31 & 12/21-12/27	1P $105-270	2P/1B $105-270	2P/2B $105-270
12/28-3/31 & 10/1-11/30	1P $160-375	2P/1B $160-375	2P/2B $160-375

4 pm check in. AE, CB, DI, DS, JC, MC, VI. Gift shop. Spacious landscaped grounds. 2 stories; exterior corridors. ▣. **Rooms:** 496; 12 2-bedroom, 2-story suites, $350-1150 for up to 4 persons. Gas fireplaces, movies, radios, data ports, honor bars, refrigerators, ⊘. **Recreation:** Pool, putting green, exercise room, massage. **Services:** Valet parking, laundry, business services. **Dining:** Restaurant; cocktail lounge; entertainment.

ARIZONA CHARLIE'S HOTEL ♦♦ Motor Inn
(702) 258-5111; FAX (702) 258-5192.
1 mi NW of I-15; Charleston Bl exit; 740 S Decatur Bl at Evergreen Av, 89107.

All year	1P $48-69	2P/1B $48-69	2P/2B $48-69

XP $4; ages 12 and under stay free. No Sat arrivals; 2-night minimum stay weekends. AE, CB, DI, DS, MC, VI. Old West atmosphere. 7 stories; interior corridors. ⅁, roll-in showers, ▣. **Rooms:** 257; luxury-level rooms. Combination/shower baths, radios, data ports, refrigerators, ⊘. **Recreation:** Small pool. **Services:** Airport transportation, laundry, business services. **Dining:** Restaurant; 24-hr room service; cocktail lounge.

BALLY'S LAS VEGAS ⊕ ♦♦♦ Hotel
(702) 739-4111; FAX (702) 794-2413.
4½ mi S on the Strip at 3645 Las Vegas Bl S; Box 96505, 89109.

Fri-Sat	1P $103-299	2P/1B $103-299	2P/2B $103-299
Sun-Thu	1P $ 99-299	2P/1B $ 99-299	2P/2B $ 99-299

XP $15; ages 17 and under stay free. Deposit required; 3-day refund notice. 2 night minimum stay weekends. AE, CB, DI, DS, JC, MC, VI. Rooms in 2 towers connected by casino and public areas. 26 stories; interior corridors. Roll-in showers. **Rooms:** 2814. Movies, radios, data ports, safes, refrigerators, ⊘. **Recreation:** Pool, sauna, steam room, whirlpool, 8 lighted tennis courts, massage, exercise room. **Services:** Valet parking, laundry, business services. **Dining:** 4 restaurants, $8-34; 2 coffee shops; buffet, $15; casino; cocktail lounge; entertainment.

BARBARY COAST HOTEL ⊕ ♦♦♦ Hotel
(702) 737-7111; FAX (702) 737-6304.
1⅛ mi S on the Strip; 3595 Las Vegas Bl S; Box 19030, 89132.

6/2-9/1	1P $49-129	2P/1B $49-129	2P/2B $49-129
9/2-6/1	1P $59-159	2P/1B $59-159	2P/2B $59-159

XP $10; ages 15 and under stay free. Deposit required. AE, CB, DI, DS, JC, MC, VI. Gay '90s decor, including large Tiffany-style stained glass mural. 5 stories; interior corridors. Roll-in showers. **Rooms:** 200; 12 suites, $200-350 for up to 2 persons. Whirlpools, movies, data ports, refrigerators, ⊘. **Services:** Laundry. **Dining:** Restaurant, $7-20; 24-hr coffee shop; casino; cocktails.

BARCELONA MOTEL ⊕ ♦♦ Motor Inn
(702) 644-6300; FAX (702) 644-6510.
7 mi NE; ½ mi from Nellis AFB, I-15 exit 48E; 5011 E Craig Rd, 89115.

1/1-1/31 &			
3/1-3/31	1P $60-65	2P/1B $65-70	2P/2B $75-80
4/1-6/30	1P $55-60	2P/1B $60-65	2P/2B $60-65
7/1-9/30	1P $40-45	2P/1B $45-50	2P/2B $45-50
10/1-12/31	1P $35-40	2P/1B $40-45	2P/2B $40-45

XP $5; ages 18 and under stay free. AE, DI, DS, MC, VI. 2 stories; exterior corridors. Roll-in showers. **Rooms:** 177. Combination/shower baths, movies, safes, microwaves, kitchens (no utensils), refrigerators, ⊘; no cable TV. **Recreation:** Small pool, whirlpool. **Services:** Laundry. **Dining:** Coffee shop, $6-10; 24-hr small casino; cocktails; entertainment.

BELLAGIO Not rated
(702) 693-7111.
On the Strip, exit I-15 at E Flamingo Av at 3600 Las Vegas Bl S, 89109.

All year	1P $159-499	2P/1B $159-499	2P/2B $159-499

Deposit required. AE, DI, DS, MC, VI. Too new to rate. Gift shop. 36 stories; interior corridors. ⓰, roll-in showers, ⓩ. **Rooms:** 3005; 1- and 2 bedroom-suites, $375-6000. Movies, radios, data ports, ⊘. **Recreation:** Pool. **Services:** Valet parking, airport transportation, laundry. **Dining:** Restaurant; cocktail lounge; entertainment.

BEST WESTERN HERITAGE INN ⊕ ♦♦♦ Motel
(702) 798-7736; (702) 798-5951.
3 blocks W of jct I-15 and Tropicana Av at 4975 S Valley View, 89118.

All year	1P $62-110	2P/1B $62-110	2P/2B $62-140

Deposit required. AE, CB, DI, DS, JC, MC. Pets $15. Gift shop. 3 stories; interior corridors. No elevators. Roll-in showers. **Rooms:** 59; 6 efficiencies; 3 kitchens; 4 whirlpool rooms $150 for up to 2 people. Movies, radios, data ports, coffeemakers, refrigerators, microwaves, ⊘. **Recreation:** Indoor pool. **Services:** Laundry, business services.

BEST WESTERN MAIN STREET INN ⓐ ♦♦ Motor Inn

(702) 382-3455; FAX (702) 382-1428.

I-15 northbound, exit 43E; I-15 southbound, exit 44E; 1000 N Main St, 89101.

All year	1P $45-135	2P/1B $45-135	2P/2B $49-135

XP $8; ages 12 and under stay free. Senior discount. AE, CB, DI, DS, MC, VI. Small pets, $8. Near downtown convention center. 2-3 stories; exterior corridors. **Rooms:** 91. Radios, refrigerators, ⊘; no cable TV. **Recreation:** Small pool. **Services:** Laundry, business services. **Dining:** 24-hr restaurant; $8-12; cocktail lounge.

BEST WESTERN MARDI GRAS INN ⓐ ♦♦ Motor Inn

(702) 731-2020; FAX (702) 731-4005.

½ mi S of convention center; 3500 Paradise Rd, 89109.

1/3-5/31 &			
9/1-11/30	1P $35-99	2P/1B $35-99	2P/2B $35-99
6/1-8/31	1P $30-99	2P/1B $30-99	2P/2B $30-99
12/1-12/28	1P $25-59	2P/1B $25-59	2P/2B $25-59
12/29-1/2	1P $50-120	2P/1B $50-120	2P/2B $50-120

XP $6; ages 18 and under stay free. Deposit required. Phone charge $1.50/day. AE, CB, DI, DS, JC, MC, VI. Gift shop. 3 stories; exterior corridors. **Rooms:** 314. Movies, data ports, coffeemakers, refrigerators, ⊘. **Recreation:** Pool, whirlpool, sun deck. **Services:** Laundry, airport transportation, business services. **Dining:** 24-hr restaurant; $9-14; slot casino; cocktails.

BEST WESTERN McCARRAN INN ⓐ ♦♦ Motel

(702) 798-5530; FAX (702) 798-7627.

I-15 exit Tropicana E toward McCarran International Airport; 4970 Paradise Rd, 89119.

Fri-Sat [CP]	1P $69-139	2P/1B $69-139	2P/2B $69-139
Sun-Thu [CP]	1P $49-129	2P/1B $49-129	2P/2B $49-129

XP $7; ages 17 and under stay free. Deposit required. Senior discount. AE, CB, DI, DS, JC, MC, VI. Located directly across from airport. 3 stories; interior corridors. **Rooms:** 99. Movies, data ports, coffeemakers, ⊘. **Recreation:** Pool, seasonal pool. **Services:** Airport/area transportation, laundry.

BEST WESTERN NELLIS MOTOR INN ⓐ ♦♦ Motel

(702) 643-6111; FAX (702) 643-8553.

7 mi NE, ³/₁₀ mi from Nellis AFB; from I-15, exit 48E; 5330 E Craig Rd, 89115.

All year	1P $48-78	2P/1B $56-89	2P/2B $56-89

XP $6; ages 12 and under stay free. Senior discount. AE, CB, DI, DS, VI. Pets, $5; $50 deposit. 2 stories; exterior corridors. **Rooms:** 52. Data ports, coffeemakers, refrigerators, ⊘. **Recreation:** Pool, playground. **Services:** Laundry. **Dining:** Coffee shop nearby.

BEST WESTERN PARKVIEW INN ⓐ ♦♦ Motel

(702) 385-1213; FAX (702) 382-2380.

8 blocks N on US 91 and 93; 905 Las Vegas Bl N, 89101.

All year	1P $42-100	2P/1B $42-100	2P/2B $49-135

XP $7-25; ages 12 and under stay free. Deposit required; 3-day notice. AE, DI, DS, JC, MC, VI. Small pets, $8. 2 stories; exterior corridors. **Rooms:** 46. Radios, ⊘; no cable TV. **Recreation:** Small pool. **Services:** Laundry.

BOULDER STATION HOTEL CASINO ⓐ ♦♦ Motel

(702) 432-7777; FAX (702) 221-6510.

411 Boulder Hwy, 89121; PO Box 12027, 89112-0027.

Fri-Sat	1P $79	2P/1B $79	2P/2B $79
Sun-Thu	1P $59	2P/1B $59	2P/2B $59

XP $10. AE, CB, DI, DS, MC, VI. Gift shop. 13 stories; interior corridors. **Rooms:** 300.

Combination/shower baths, movies, data ports, coffeemakers, refrigerators, ⊘. **Recreation:** Pool. **Services:** Airport/area transportation, business services. **Dining:** Restaurant; cocktail lounge.

CAESARS PALACE
♦♦♦♦ Hotel
(702) 731-7110; FAX (702) 731-6636.

On the strip, exit I-15 at E Flamingo Rd at 3570 Las Vegas Bl S, 89109.

All year	1P $100-175	2P/1B $115-190	2P/2B $115-190

XP $20. Deposit required. AE, CB, DI, DS, JC, MC, VI. Large rooms. Attractively landscaped grounds & marble statuary. Mall offers shops, art galleries and eateries. 29 stories; interior corridors. Roll-in showers, ⌼. **Rooms:** 2700. Movies, VCRs, radios, data ports, refrigerators, ⊘. **Recreation:** Pool, 3 lighted tennis courts. **Services:** Valet parking, laundry, business services. **Dining:** Restaurants; 24-hr room service; cocktail lounge; entertainment.

CALIFORNIA HOTEL
♦♦ Hotel
(702) 385-1222; FAX (702) 388-2660.

In downtown casino center area at 1st and Ogden; Box 630, 89125.

Fri-Sat	1P $50-80	2P/1B $50-80	2P/2B $50-80
Sun-Thu	1P $40-65	2P/1B $40-65	2P/2B $40-65

XP $5. Deposit required. Senior discount. AE, CB, DI, DS, MC, VI. "Aloha"-style decor. Gift shop. 23 stories; interior corridors. Roll-in showers, ⌼. **Rooms:** 781. Combination/shower baths, movies, safes, refrigerators, ⊘. **Recreation:** Pool. **Services:** Valet parking, business services. **Dining** Restaurant; cocktail lounge.

CARRIAGE HOUSE ⓐⓐⓐ
♦♦♦ Condo Hotel
(702) 798-1020; FAX (702) 798-1020.

1 block E off the Strip; 105 E Harmon Av, 89109.

All year	1P $89-145	2P/1B $89-145	2P/2B 89-165

Deposit required. Senior discount. AE, CB, DI, DS, MC, VI. 9 stories; interior corridors. Roll-in showers. **Rooms:** 155; 15 2-bedroom units, $275-525 for 2-6 persons; 41 efficiencies; 114 kitchens. Combination/shower baths, movies, VCRs, data ports, safes, microwaves, ⊘. **Recreation:** Pool, whirlpool, 1 lighted tennis court. **Services:** Laundry, airport transportation, business services. **Dining:** Kiefer's Atop the Carriage House, see listing; cocktail lounge. **(See ad below.)**

CIRCUS CIRCUS HOTEL
♦♦ Hotel
(702) 734-0410; FAX (702) 734-5897.

2⅓ mi S on the Strip at 2880 Las Vegas Bl S; Box 14967, 89114.

Fri-Sat	1P $49-119	2P/1B $49-119	2P/2B $49-119
Sun-Thu	1P $29- 89	2P/1B $29- 89	2P/2B $29- 89

XP $10-30. Deposit required. AE, CB, DI, DS, MC, VI. Gift shop. Hotel towers; motel rooms in 3-story building. 2-29 stories; interior corridors. 🛗, roll-in showers, 🔲. **Rooms:** 3744. Combination/shower baths, movies, data ports, safes, refrigerators, ⊘. **Recreation:** Pools. **Services:** Valet parking, laundry, business services. **Dining:** Restaurant; cocktail lounge.

CLUB HOTEL BY DOUBLETREE LAS VEGAS AIRPORT   Not Rated
(702) 948-4000; FAX (702) 948-4100.
I-215, exit Warm Springs Rd. 7250 Pollock Dr, 89119.

Fri-Sat	1P $ 89	2P/1B $ 89	2P/2B $ 89
Sun-Thu	1P $119	2P/1B $119	2P/2B $119

XP $15; ages 18 and under stay free. AE, CB, DI, DS, MC, VI. Too new to rate. Pets. 6 stories; interior corridors. Roll-in showers. **Rooms:** 190. Combination/shower baths, movies, radios, data ports, coffeemakers, ⊘. **Recreation:** Pool. **Services:** Airport transportation, laundry, business services.

COMFORT INN ⦿   ♦♦♦ Motel
(702) 399-1500; FAX (702) 399-2900.
I-15 exit Cheyenne West; 910 E Cheyenne Av, 89030.

Fri-Sat [CP]	1P $69-79	2P/1B $69-79	2P/2B $69-79
Sun-Thu [CP]	1P $59-69	2P/1B $59-69	2P/2B $59-69

XP $10; ages 18 and under stay free. AE, CB, DI, DS, MC, VI. Small pets, $10. Gift shop. 3 stories; interior corridors; no elevator. **Rooms:** 59; 3 kitchens; 3 whirlpool rooms. Combination/shower baths, movies, radios, refrigerators, microwaves, ⊘. **Recreation:** Pool, whirlpool, sauna. **Services:** Laundry. **Dining:** Coffee shop nearby.

COMFORT INN CENTRAL ⦿   ♦♦ Motel
(702) 733-7800; FAX (702) 733-7353.
From I-15 exit Flamingo Rd E at Koval Rd; 211 E Flamingo Rd, 89109.

Fri-Sat [CP]	1P $65	2P/1B $75	2P/2B $85
Sun-Thu [CP]	1P $55	2P/1B $65	2P/2B $75

XP $5; ages 16 and under stay free. Senior discount. AE, CB, DI, DS, JC, MC, VI. 2 stories; exterior corridors. **Rooms:** 121; 4 2-bedroom units. Movies, radios, ⊘. **Recreation:** Pool. **Dining:** Restaurant nearby.

COMFORT INN SOUTH ⦿   ♦♦ Motel
(702) 736-3600; FAX (702) 736-0726.
½ mi E of I-15, Tropicana Av exit; 5075 S Koval Ln, 89109.

Fri-Sat [CP]	1P $65-85	2P/1B $65-85	2P/2B $65-85
Sun-Thu [CP]	1P $42-65	2P/1B $42-65	2P/2B $42-65

XP $5; ages 18 and under stay free. Senior discount. AE, CB, DI, DS, JC, MC, VI. 2 stories; exterior corridors. **Rooms:** 106. Movies, ⊘. **Recreation:** Pool. **Services:** Laundry.

COURTYARD BY MARRIOTT-CONVENTION CENTER   ♦♦♦ Motor Inn
(702) 791-3600; FAX (702) 796-7981.
Just E of the Strip, 1 block to convention center; 3275 Paradise Rd, 89109.

All year	1P $89-135	2P/1B $89-135	2P/2B $89-135

Rates for up to 5 persons. AE, CB, DI, DS, JC, MC, VI. 3 stories; interior corridors. **Rooms:** 149. Movies, coffeemaker, radio, refrigerators, data ports, ⊘; no cable TV. **Recreation:** Pool, exercise room. **Services:** Laundry, airport transportation, business services. **Dining:** Restaurant.

CROWNE PLAZA ⦿   ♦♦♦ Motor Inn
(702) 369-4400; FAX (702) 369-3770.
Exit I-15 Flamingo, ½ mi E to Paradise, S to 4255 S Paradise Rd, 89109.

2/1-6/30 & 9/1-1/31	1P $125-145	2P/1B $125-145	2P/2B $125-145
7/1-8/31	1P $ 95	2P/1B $ 95	2P/2B $ 95

XP $15; ages 18 and under stay free. Senior discount. AE, CB, DI, DS, JC, MC, VI. Pets, $200 deposit; on first floor only. Atrium lobby, vibrant colors, cascading fountains. 6 stories; interior corridors. ♿, ▨. **Rooms:** 201. Movies, radios, data ports, coffeemakers, refrigerators, ⊘. **Recreation:** Pool, whirlpool, sauna, exercise room. **Services:** Laundry, airport transportation, business services. **Dining:** Restaurant, 6 am-10 pm, $8-16; cocktail lounge.

DAYS INN-AIRPORT ♦♦ Motel
(702) 740-4040; FAX (702) 736-8295.
Exit I-15 at E Tropicana Av, 1⅕ mi E to Paradise Rd, ½ mi S to 5125 Swenson St, 89119.

Fri-Sat	1P $65-145	2P/1B $65-145	2P/2B $65-145
Sun-Thu	1P $45-125	2P/1B $45-125	2P/2B $45-125

AE, CB, DI, DS, MC, VI. 2 stories; exterior corridors. **Rooms:** 183. Radios, microwaves, refrigerators, ⊘. **Recreation:** Pool. **Services:** Airport/area transportation, laundry.

DAYS INN DOWNTOWN ⒶⒶⒶ ♦♦ Motel
(702) 388-1400; FAX (702) 388-9622.
On US 93 and 95 business rte; 707 E Fremont St, 89101.

Fri-Sat 2/1-11/14 &			
1/2-1/31	1P $ 50-120	2P/1B $ 60-120	2P/2B $ 60-120
Sun-Thu 2/1-11/14,			
4/2-1/31 &			
11/22-12/26	1P $ 36-100	2P/1B $ 46-100	2P/2B $ 46-100
11/15-11/21 &			
12/27-1/1	1P $110-150	2P/1B $110-150	2P/2B $120-175

XP $10; ages 16 and under stay free. AE, CB, DI, DS, JC, MC, VI. 3 stories; exterior corridors. **Rooms:** 147 rooms; few small rooms, some large; 7 1-bedroom suites, $60-120. Movies, ⊘. **Recreation:** Pool. **Dining:** Restaurant, 7 am-7 pm, Sat and Sun to noon.

THE DESERT INN ♦♦♦♦ Resort Complex
(702) 733-4444; FAX (702) 733-4774.
On the Strip; I-15 NB exit E Flamingo Av, SB exit E Sahara Av; 3145 Las Vegas Bl S, 89109.

All year [CP]	1P $195-275	2P/1B $195-275	2P/2B $195-275

XP $35; ages 17 and under stay free. Deposit required; 3-day refund notice. AE, CB, DI, DS, JC, MC, VI. Gift shop. Lavishly landscaped grounds. 14 stories; interior corridors. Roll-in showers. **Rooms:** 715; 284 whirlpool suites, $1500-5000 for up to 2 persons. Combination/shower bath, movies, radios, data ports, safes, refrigerators, ⊘. **Recreation:** Pool, 4 lighted tennis courts, 18 holes golf, exercise room, massage. **Services:** Valet parking, laundry, business services. **Dining:** Restaurant; 24-hr room service; cocktail lounge; name entertainment.

ECONO LODGE-DOWNTOWN ⒶⒶⒶ ♦ Motel
(702) 384-8211; FAX (702) 384-8580.
Exit I-15 downtown casino center; 520 S Casino Center Bl, 89101.

Fri-Sat	1P $50	2P/1B $50	2P/2B $60
Sun-Thu	1P $40	2P/1B $40	2P/2B $50

XP $10. Ages 18 and under stay free. Deposit required. Senior discount. AE, CB, DI, DS, JC, MC, VI. 3 stories; interior corridors. **Rooms:** 48; 4 1-bedroom apartments, $69-95 for up to 4 persons; 4 kitchens, no utensils. Movies, coffeemakers, refrigerators, ⊘. **Services:** Laundry.

EMERALD SPRINGS-HOLIDAY INN ⒶⒶⒶ ♦♦♦ Motor Inn
(702) 732-9100; FAX (702) 731-9784.
I-15 exit E Flamingo Rd; 325 E Flamingo Rd, 89109.

All year	1P $79-99	2P/1B $79-99	2P/2B $79-99

XP $15; ages 19 and under stay free. Deposit required. Monthly rates. Senior discount. AE, CB, DI, DS, JC, MC, VI. 3 stories; interior corridors. **Rooms:** 150; 16 suites with wet bar and whirlpool tub, $99-250 for up to 2 persons. Movies, VCRs, video games, data ports, coffeemakers, refrigerators, microwaves, ⊘. **Recreation:** Pool, whirlpool, exercise room. **Services:** Airport/area transportation (Strip 7 am-11 pm), laundry, business services. **Dining:** Restaurant, Sun-Mon 6 am-10 pm, Fri-Sat to 11 pm, $10-20; cocktail lounge.

EXCALIBUR HOTEL & CASINO ◆◆◆ Hotel
(702) 597-7777; FAX (702) 597-7009.
I-15 exit E Tropicana Av; 3850 Las Vegas Bl S; Box 96778, 89193.
All year   1P $55-220   2P/1B $55-220   2P/2B $55-220
XP $10; ages 17 and under stay free. AE, CB, DI, DS, JC, MC, VI. Medieval castle theme. 28 stories; interior corridors. ♿, roll-in showers, ▨. **Rooms:** 4008; 48 whirlpool rooms. Shower baths, movies, refrigerators, ⊘; no cable TV. **Recreation:** Pool. **Services:** Valet parking, laundry. **Dining:** Restaurant; 24-hr room service; cocktail lounge; entertainment.

FAIRFIELD INN BY MARRIOTT ◆◆ Motel
(702) 791-0899; FAX (702) 791-2705.
I-15 exit E Flamingo Rd; 3 blocks N of convention center; 3850 Paradise Rd, 89109.
2/1-3/13 &
4/23-11/1 [CP]   1P $62- 95   2P/1B $62- 95   2P/2B $62- 95
3/14-4/22 [CP]   1P $62-125   2P/1B $62-125   2P/2B $62-125
11/2-1/31 [CP]   1P $62-175   2P/1B $62-175   2P/2B $62-175
Rates for up to 4 persons. Senior discount. AE, DI, DS, MC, VI. Large lobby with many tables and chairs; comfortable rooms. 4 stories; interior corridors. ▨. **Rooms:** 129. Movies, radios, ⊘. **Recreation:** Pool. **Services:** Airport transportation, business services. **Dining:** Restaurant nearby.

FIESTA CASINO HOTEL ◆◆ Motor Inn
(702) 631-7000; FAX (702) 631-7070.
3 mi N of downtown at 2400 N Rancho Dr, 89130.
All year   1P $39   2P/1B $42   2P/2B $45
XP $5. AE, DI, DS, MC, VI. 5 stories; interior corridors. **Rooms:** 100. Radios, ⊘. **Recreation:** Pool. **Dining:** Restaurant; cocktail lounge.

FLAMINGO HILTON-LAS VEGAS ⏺ ◆◆◆ Hotel
(702) 733-3111; FAX (702) 733-3528.
From I-15, exit Flamingo Rd E, then N on The Strip; 3555 Las Vegas Bl S, 89109.
All year   1P $69-279   2P/1B $69-279   2P/2B $69-279
XP $20; ages 18 and under stay free. AE, CB, DI, DS, MC, VI. 2-28 stories; interior corridors. Roll-in showers. **Rooms:** 3642; suites, $250-5800 for up to 2 persons. Movies, data ports, safes, refrigerators, ⊘. **Recreation:** 2 pools, whirlpools, 4 lighted tennis courts, exercise room, massage. **Services:** Valet parking, laundry, business services. **Dining:** 5 restaurants; cafeteria; 24-hr coffee shop; $7-20; buffet $6-9; 24-hr room service; casino; cocktail lounge; entertainment. **(See ad next page.)**

FOUR SEASON HOTEL LAS VEGAS Not Rated
(702) 632-5000; FAX (702) 632-5222.
I-15, E Tropicana exit, S on the Strip at 3950 Las Vegas Bl S, 89119.
Under construction. Scheduled to open in March of 1999. **Rooms:** 424.

GOLD COAST HOTEL ◆◆◆ Hotel
(702) 367-7111; (702) 367-8575.
1 block W of I-15, exit Flamingo Rd W to 4000 W Flamingo Rd; Box 80750, Las Vegas, 89180.
All year   1P $29-175   2P/1B $29-175   2P/2B $29-175

XP $5; ages 16 and under stay free. Deposit required. Senior discount. AE, CB, DI, DS, JC, MC, VI. Gift shop. Colonial-Spanish architecture. 10 stories; interior corridors. **Rooms:** 711; 18 beautifully decorated suites with wet bar and refrigerator, $150-300 for 2 persons. Combination/shower baths, movies, radios, ∅. **Recreation:** Pool. **Services:** Valet parking, laundry, child care, business services. **Dining:** Restaurant; 24-hr room service; cocktail lounge; entertainment.

GOLDEN NUGGET HOTEL ⏣ ◆◆◆◆ Hotel
(702) 385-7111; FAX (702) 386-8362.
In the downtown casino center area at 129 E Fremont St; Box 610 Las Vegas, 89125.

All year	1P $59-299	2P/1B $59-299	2P/2B $59-299

XP $20. Deposit required. AE, DI, DS, MC, VI. Large rooms, attractive contemporary decor. Video arcade. 10-22 stories; interior corridors. ♿, 🖵. **Rooms:** 1907; 1- and 2-bedroom suites, $275-375 for 2 persons. **Rooms:** Radios. **Recreation:** Pool, whirlpool, massage, exercise room. **Services:** Valet parking, laundry, business services. **Dining:** 2 dining rooms; restaurant; coffee shop; 24-hr buffet; $10-35; casino; 24-hr room service; cocktail lounge; entertainment.

HARRAH'S-LAS VEGAS ◆◆◆ Hotel
(702) 369-5000; FAX (702) 369-5008.
4 mi S on the Strip; 3475 Las Vegas Bl S, 89109.

All year	1P $50-259	2P/1B $50-259	2P/2B $50-259

XP $10; ages 12 and under stay free. Deposit required; 3-day refund notice. AE, CB, DI, DS, JC, MC, VI. Gift shop. 15-35 stories; interior corridors. ♿, roll-in showers, 🖵. **Rooms:** 2683 rooms; 64 suites, $195-350 for up to 2 persons. Movies, radios, ∅. **Recreation:** Pool, whirlpool, exercise room, massage. **Services:** Valet parking, laundry, child care, business services. **Dining:** Restaurants; cocktail lounge; entertainment.

HAWTHORN SUITES – LAS VEGAS

♦♦♦ Suite Motor Inn
(702) 739-7000; FAX (702) 739-9350.

Exit I-15 at E Tropicana Av, ⅛ mi E to Duke Ellington Wy, S to 5051 Duke Ellington Wy, 89119.

All year [BP]	1P $99-169	2P/1B $99-169	2P/2B $99-169

Senior discount. AE, CB, DI, DS, JC, MC, VI. 3 stories; exterior corridors. ⧅. **Rooms:** 284. All suites include separate bedroom, living room and full kitchen. Radios, data ports, coffeemakers, microwaves, ⊘. **Recreation:** Pool. **Services:** Laundry, business services. **Dining:** Restaurant nearby.

HILTON GRAND VACATIONS CLUB

♦♦♦ Hotel
(702) 697-2900; FAX (702) 697-2910.

Exit I-15 Flamingo E, N on Strip; directly behind Flamingo Hilton; 3575 Las Vegas Bl S, 89109.

All year	1P $109-199	2P/1B $109-199	2P/2B $239-399

4 pm check in. Deposit required; 3-day refund notice. AE, DI, DS, MC, VI. Attractively landscaped grounds and public areas. 17 stories; interior corridors. Roll-in showers. **Rooms:** 291; 214 2-bedroom units; 146 efficiencies; 145 kitchens. Movies, VCRs, radios, data ports, ⊘. **Recreation:** Pool. **Services:** Valet parking, laundry.

HOLIDAY INN CASINO BOARDWALK

♦♦♦ Hotel
(702) 735-2400; FAX (702) 735-8152.

I-15 exit Flamingo Bl, S on Strip to 3750 Las Vegas Bl S, 89109.

Fri-Sat	1P $79-239	2P/1B $79-239	2P/2B $79-239
Sun-Thu	1P $49-239	2P/1B $49-239	2P/2B $49-239

XP $15; ages 19 and under stay free. AE, CB, DI, DS, JC, MC, VI. Gift shop. 4-16 stories; interior/exterior corridors. Roll-in showers. **Rooms:** 653. Movies, radios, data ports, ⊘. **Recreation:** Pool. **Services:** Business services. **Dining:** Restaurant; $7-10; cocktail lounge.

HOLIDAY INN EXPRESS ⏺

♦♦♦ Motel
(702) 256-3766; FAX (702) 256-3763.

I-15 exit Sahara, 6½ mi W to 8669 W Sahara Av, 89117.

Fri-Sat[CP]	1P $99-250	2P/1B $99-250	2P/2B $99-250
Sun-Thu [CP]	1P $89-250	2P/1B $89-250	2P/2B $89-250

XP $10-20; ages 18 and under stay free. Deposit required. Senior discount. AE, DI, DS, MC, VI. Pets. 3 stories; interior corridors. **Rooms:** 59; 14 efficiencies, 3 kitchens, 3 whirlpool rooms. Combination/shower baths, movies, radios, data ports, refrigerators, microwaves, ⊘. **Recreation:** Indoor pool, whirlpool. **Services:** Laundry. **Dining:** Restaurant nearby.

HOLIDAY INN FITZGERALDS CASINO

♦♦♦ Motel
(702) 388-2400; FAX (702) 388-2181.

In downtown casino center; 301 Fremont St, 89101.

Fri-Sat	1P $50-120	2P/1B $50-120	2P/2B $50-120
Sun-Thu	1P $34- 80	2P/1B $34- 80	2P/2B $34- 80

XP $10; ages 18 and under stay free. Deposit required. Senior discount. AE, CB, DI, DS, MC, VI. Gift shop. 34 stories; interior corridors. **Rooms:** 638; 34 whirlpool rooms. Movies, radios, refrigerators, ⊘. **Services:** Business services. **Dining:** Restaurant; cocktail lounge.

HOWARD JOHNSON HOTEL & CASINO ⏺

♦♦ Hotel
(702) 798-1111; FAX (702) 798-7138.

Adjacent to I-15, Tropicana W exit; 3111 W Tropicana Av, 89103.

Fri-Sat	1P $89	2P/1B $89	2P/2B $89
Sun-Thu	1P $59	2P/1B $59	2P/2B $59

XP $10; ages 12 and under stay free. AE, DI, DS, MC, VI. Deposit required. Convenient to airport and Strip. 6 stories; interior corridors. **Rooms:** 150. Movies, radios, coffeemakers, refrigerators, ⊘. **Recreation:** Pool, whirlpool. **Services:** Airport transportation. **Dining:** 24-hr coffee shop; $6-12; cocktail lounge.

HOWARD JOHNSON INN – AIRPORT ♦ Motel
(702) 798-2777; FAX (702) 736-8295.
Exit I-15, E Tropicana Exit, 1⅛ mi to Paradise Rd, ³⁄₁₀ mi S to 5100 Paradise Rd, 89119.

Fri-Sat	1P $65-145	2P/1B $65-145	2P/2B $65-145
Sun-Thu	1P $45-125	2P/1B $45-125	2P/2B $45-125

Deposit required. AE, CB, DI, DS, MC. 2 stories; exterior corridors. **Rooms:** 144. Radios, refrigerators, microwaves, ⊘. **Recreation:** Pool. **Services:** Laundry, airport transportation, business services. **Dining:** Restaurant; cocktail lounge.

LA QUINTA INN ♦♦♦ Motel
(702) 739-7457; FAX (702) 736-1129.
5½ mi S on Strip at 3782 Las Vegas Bl S, 89109-4312.

2/1-4/30 &			
12/31-1/31[CP]	1P $69-89	2P/1B $69-89	2P/2B $69-89
5/1-1/31 [CP]	1P $55-72	2P/1B $55-72	2P/2B $55-72

AE, CB, DI, DS, JC, MC, VI. Pets. Spanish exterior design. 3 stories; exterior corridors. **Rooms:** 114. Movies, radios, data ports, ⊘. **Recreation:** Pool. **Services:** Airport transportation. **Dining:** Restaurant nearby. **(See ad below.)**

LA QUINTA INN CONVENTION CENTER ⏺ ♦♦♦ Motel
(702) 796-9000; FAX (702) 796-3537.
⅛ mi S of convention center, exit I-15 Flamingo Av E, ½ mi E of the Strip; 3970 Paradise Rd, 89109.

2/1-4/30 [CP]	1P $69-89	2P/1B $69-89	2P/2B $69-89
5/1-1/31 [CP]	1P $52-72	2P/1B $52-72	2P/2B $52-72

AE, CB, DI, DS, JC, MC, VI. 3 stories; interior corridors. **Rooms:** 228; 9 2-bedroom units. Some units with balconies, few with patios. Movies, radios, data ports, coffeemakers, refrigerators, microwaves, ⊘. **Recreation:** Pool, whirlpool. **Services:** Laundry, airport transportation, business services. **Dining:** Restaurant nearby. **(See ad above.)**

LAS VEGAS HILTON ⏺ ♦♦♦♦ Hotel
(702) 732-5111; FAX (702) 732-5805.
Exit I-15 at Sahara, 2 mi E, adjacent to convention center; 3000 Paradise Rd; Box 93147, 89193.

All year	1P $95-275	2P/1B $95-275	2P/2B $95-275

XP $20. Deposit required; 3-day refund notice. AE, CB, DI, DS, JC, MC, VI. Video arcade. 30 stories; interior corridors. 🛗, roll-in showers, 📷.. **Rooms:** 3174; 300 suites, $310-1250 for up to 2 persons; luxury-level rooms. Movies, radios, data ports, safes, refrigerators, ⊘. **Recreation:** Pool, whirlpools, 6 lighted tennis courts, putting green, exercise room. **Services:** Valet parking, laundry, business services. **Dining:** 8 dining rooms; 24-hr coffee shop, $8-35; buffet, $9-13; 24-hr room service; cocktail lounge; Andiamo, see separate listing.

LUXOR LAS VEGAS (AAA)   ♦♦♦ Resort Hotel
(702) 262-4444; FAX (702) 262-4454.
I-15 exit E Tropicana, just S on the Strip; 3900 Las Vegas Bl S; Box 98640, 89193.
All year   1P $59-259   2P/1B $59-259   2P/2B $59-259
XP $15; ages 12 and younger stay free. AE, CB, DI, DS, JC, MC, VI. Gift shop. 350-foot glass-faced pyramid, crowned by a 40-billion candlepower vertical light beam. Egyptian decor theme. Special effects attractions, Virtualand arcade and King Tut's Tomb and Museum (see listing, *LasVegas Valley*) within the atrium, 3-D Imax theater. 30 stories; interior corridors. ⬤, roll-in showers, 🗹. **Rooms:** 4526. Combination/shower baths, movies, radios, data ports, ⊘. **Recreation:** Pool, wading pool, whirlpools, sauna, massage, exercise room. **Services:** Valet parking, laundry, airport transportation, business services. **Dining:** 2 dining rooms, 4 restaurants, coffee shop, deli, food court; $10-50; 24-hr room service; cocktail lounge; entertainment; night club.

MAIN STREET STATION   ♦♦♦ Hotel
(702) 387-1896; FAX (702) 386-4466.
In downtown casino center, 200 N Main St, 89125.
All year   1P $50-125   2P/1B $50-125   2P/2B $50-125
Check-in 4 p.m. AE, CB, DI, DS, MC, VI. Gift shop. 17 stories; interior corridors. Roll-in showers. **Rooms:** 406. Combination/shower baths, movies, data ports, ⊘. **Services:** Business services. **Dining:** Restaurant.

MGM GRAND HOTEL CASINO & THEME PARK ♦♦♦ Resort Hotel
(702) 891-1111; FAX (702) 891-1030.
I-15 exit E Tropicana Av; 3799 Las Vegas Bl S, 89109.
All year   1P $69-259   2P/1B $69-259   2P/2B $69-259
XP $25; ages 12 and under stay free. Deposit required. AE, CB, DI, DS, JC, MC, VI. Gift shop. World's largest hotel; 33-acre theme park. 30 stories; interior corridors. ⬤, roll-in showers, 🗹. **Rooms:** 5005; 400 suites, $169-500 for up to 2 persons. Movies, radios, ⊘. **Recreation:** Heated pool, 5 lighted tennis courts, exercise room, massage. **Services:** Valet parking, laundry, business services. **Dining:** Restaurant.

THE MIRAGE   ♦♦♦♦ Resort Hotel
(702) 791-7111; FAX (702) 791-7446.
3½ mi S on the Strip; 3400 Las Vegas Bl S, 89109.
Fri-Sat   1P $109-399   2P/1B $109-399   2P/2B $109-399
Sun-Thu   1P $ 79-399   2P/1B $ 79-399   2P/2B $ 79-399
XP $30. Deposit required. AE, DI, DS, JC, MC, VI. Lavish grounds and unique public areas; home to Siegfried and Roy and their white tigers, also dolphin habitat. Free tram to Treasure Island. 30 stories; interior corridors. ⬤, roll-in showers, 🗹. **Rooms:** 3044; 1- and 2-bedroom suites, $300-950 for 2 persons. Movies, VCRs, radios, refrigerators, data ports, safes, ⊘. **Recreation:** Pool, exercise room, massage. **Services:** Valet parking, area transportation, business services. **Dining:** Restaurant; cocktail lounge; entertainment.

MONTE CARLO RESORT & CASINO   ♦♦♦ Hotel
(702) 730-7777; FAX (702) 730-7250.
On the Strip between Flamingo Rd & Tropicana Av; 3770 Las Vegas Bl S, 89109.
Fri-Sat   1P $109-249   2P/1B $109-249   2P/2B $109-249
Sun-Thu   1P $ 69-199   2P/1B $ 69-199   2P/2B $ 69-199
XP $15; ages 13 and under stay free. Deposit required; 3-day refund notice. AE, DI, DS, MC, VI. 32 stories; interior corridors. Roll-in showers, 🗹. **Rooms:** 3014; 203 with whirlpool. Movies, radios, data ports, ⊘. **Recreation:** Pool, exercise room, 3 lighted tennis courts, massage. **Services:** Valet parking, laundry, business services. **Dining:** Restaurants; 24-hr room service.

THE ORLEANS

♦♦♦ Hotel
(702) 365-7111; FAX (702) 365-7505.
Exit I-15 at Tropicana, 1 mi W to 4500 W Tropicana, 89103.

Fri-Sat	1P $89-109	2P/1B $89-109	2P/2B $89-109
Sun-Thu	1P $49-69	2P/1B $49-69	2P/2B $49-69

XP $10. Deposit required. AE, CB, DI, DS, JC, MC, VI. Gift shop. 22 stories. Roll-in showers. **Rooms:** 840. Combination/shower baths, movies, data ports, ⊘. **Recreation:** Pool. **Services:** Child care, business services. **Dining:** Restaurant; cocktail lounge; entertainment.

PALACE STATION HOTEL & CASINO ⚠

♦♦♦ Hotel
(702) 367-2411; FAX (702) 367-2478.
SW corner of Sahara & Rancho at 2411 W Sahara Av, 89102.

Fri-Sat	1P $79-149	2P/1B $79-149	2P/2B $79-149
Sun-Thu	1P $39- 99	2P/1B $39- 99	2P/2B $39- 99

XP $10-15; ages 17 and under stay free. AE, CB, DI, DS, MC, VI. Gift shop. 20 stories, interior corridors. ⧄. **Rooms:** 573. Movies, VCRs, radios, data ports, safes, coffeemakers, refrigerators, microwaves, ⊘. **Recreation:** Pool. **Services:** Valet parking, laundry, airport/area transportation, business services. **Dining:** Restaurant.

QUALITY INN & KEY LARGO CASINO

♦♦ Hotel
(702) 733-7777; FAX (702) 369-6911.
377 E Flamingo Rd, 89109.

All year	1P $39-200	2P/1B $39-200	2P/2B $39-200

XP $10-15; ages 18 and under stay free. Senior discount. AE, CB, DI, DS, MC, VI. Gift shop. Attractively landscaped grounds. 3 stories; interior/exterior corridors. ⧄. **Rooms:** 315. Movies, radios, data ports, coffeemakers, refrigerators, ⊘. **Recreation:** Pool, whirlpool. **Services:** Airport/area transportation, laundry, business services. **Dining:** Restaurant; 24 hrs; $4-13; cocktail lounge.

RESIDENCE INN BY MARRIOTT

♦♦♦ Apartment Hotel
(702) 796-9300; FAX (702) 796-9562.
Opposite convention center; 3225 Paradise Rd, 89109.

All year [CP]	1P $95-319	2P/1B $95-319	2P/2B $125-329

4 pm check in. Deposit required. AE, CB, DI, DS, JC, MC, VI. Pets. 2 stories; exterior corridors. **Rooms:** 192; 48 2-bedroom units. Movies, VCRs, data ports, kitchens, microwaves, ⊘. **Recreation:** Pool. **Services:** Airport transportation, laundry, business services. **Dining:** Complimentary snacks and beverages weekdays 5:30-7 pm.

RIO SUITE HOTEL & CASINO

♦♦♦ Hotel
(702) 252-7777; FAX (702) 252-8909.
Exit I-15 at Flamingo Rd, ³⁄₁₀ mi W; 3700 W Flamingo Rd, 89103; Box 14160, 89114.

All year	1P $95-149	2P/1B $95-149	2P/2B $95-149

XP $15. AE, CB, DI, DS, JC, MC, VI. Gift shop. Tropical swim lagoon with white sand. Masquerade village live carnival parade and show. 41 stories; interior corridors. ♿, roll-in showers, ⧄. **Rooms:** 2550; specialty suites, $300-850. Combination/shower bath, movies, data ports, coffeemakers, refrigerators, ⊘. **Recreation:** Pool, massage, exercise room. **Services:** Valet parking, laundry, business services. **Dining:** Restaurants; 24-hr room service; entertainment.

RIVIERA HOTEL

♦♦ Hotel
(702) 734-5110; FAX (702) 794-9451.
From I-15, exit E Sahara; 2901 Las Vegas Bl S, 89109.

All year	1P $59-145	2P/1B $59-145	2P/2B $59-145

XP $20. Deposit required. AE, CB, DI, DS, JC, MC, VI. Gift shop. Wedding chapel. 24 stories; interior corridors. ⧄. **Rooms:** 2073; many large rooms. Movies, radios, safes, refrigerators, ⊘. **Recreation:** Pool, 2 lighted tennis courts, massage, exercise room. **Services:** Valet parking, laundry, business services. **Dining:** Restaurant; cocktail lounge; entertainment.

ST. TROPEZ ALL SUITE HOTEL ◍ ◆◆◆ Complex
(702) 369-5400; FAX (702) 369-1150.
2 mi S of convention center at Paradise Rd; 455 E Harmon Av, 89109.
All year [CP]   1P $95-115   2P/1B $115-125   2P/2B $115-125
XP $10; ages 18 and under stay free. Senior discount. AE, DI, DS, MC, VI. Gift shop. Surrounding attractively landscaped grounds. 2 stories; interior/exterior corridors. Roll-in showers, 🖻. **Rooms:** 149; courtyard units with patio or deck; 34 whirlpool units, $135-180 for up to 2 persons. Combination/shower baths, movies, VCRs, radios, data ports, safes, coffeemakers, refrigerators, ⊘. **Recreation:** Pool, whirlpool, exercise room. **Services:** Airport/area transportation, laundry, business services. **Dining:** Restaurant nearby; cocktail lounge.

SAM'S TOWN HOTEL ◆◆◆ Hotel
(702) 456-7777; FAX (702) 454-8014.
1 mi E of I-515 and SR 93/95, Flamingo exit; 5111 Boulder Hwy, 89122.
Fri-Sat   1P $75-100   2P/1B $75-155   2P/2B $75-155
Sun-Thu   1P $50- 65   2P/1B $50- 80   2P/2B $50- 80
XP $5; ages 12 and under stay free. Deposit required. AE, CB, DI, DS, MC, VI. Gift shop. Central indoor park with waterfall; nightly laser and water show. Southwestern decor. 9 stories; interior corridors. Roll-in showers. **Rooms:** 650. Movies, radios, refrigerators, ⊘. **Recreation:** Pool. **Services:** Valet parking, area transportation, business services. **Dining:** Restaurant; 24-hr room service; cocktail lounge; entertainment.

SILVERTON HOTEL & CASINO ◆◆ Hotel
(702) 263-7777; FAX (702) 896-5635.
I-15 exit 33 W to 3333 Blue Diamond Rd, 89139.
Fri-Sat   1P $70   2P/1B $70   2P/2B $70
Sun-Thu   1P $49   2P/1B $49   2P/2B $49
XP $5. AE, CB, DI, DS, MC, VI. Gift shop. Replica of an 1800's Old West frontier mining town. 4 stories; interior corridors. **Rooms:** 300; 12 suites with whirlpool, $150-195 for up to 2 persons. Radios, data ports, ⊘. **Recreation:** Pool. **Services:** Area transportation, laundry, child care, business services. **Dining:** Restaurant; entertainment.

SOMERSET HOUSE MOTEL ◍ ◆◆ Motor Inn
(702) 735-4411; FAX (702) 369-2388.
3 mi S, 1 block E off the Strip. 1 block from convention center; 294 Convention Center Dr, 89109.
Fri-Sat   1P $40   2P/1B $50   2P/2B $50
Sun-Thu   1P $32   2P/1B $40   2P/2B $40
XP $5; ages 12 and under stay free. Deposit required; 3-day refund notice. Senior discount. AE, CB, DI, MC, VI. Weekly rates available. 3 stories; interior/exterior corridors. 🖔, roll-in showers. **Rooms:** 104; 17 efficiencies; 63 kitchens. Balconies, combination/shower baths, movies, radios, refrigerators, ⊘; no cable TV. **Recreation:** Pool. **Services:** Laundry, business services.

TEXAS STATION GAMBLING HALL & HOTEL ◍ ◆◆◆ Motor Inn
(702) 631-1000; FAX (702) 631-8120.
On Business US 95, 3 mi N of downtown at 2101 Texas Star Ln, 89030.
Fri-Sat   1P $99-129   2P/1B $99-129   2P/2B $99-129
Sun-Thu   1P $59- 79   2P/1B $59- 79   2P/2B $59- 79
XP $10-15; ages 13 and under stay free. Deposit required; handling fee imposed. AE, CB, DI, DS, MC, VI. 6 stories; interior corridors. **Rooms:** 200. Radios, safes, coffeemakers, refrigerators, ⊘. **Recreation:** Pool. **Dining:** Restaurant; cocktail lounge.

TRAVELODGE-WEST SAHARA   ♦♦ Motor Inn
(702) 733-0001; FAX (702) 733-1571.
E off I-15, just W of the Strip; Westbound Sahara traffic exit right via Western Av; 1501 W Sahara Av, 89102.

Fri-Sat	1P $59- 89	2P/1B $59- 89	2P/2B $59- 89
Sun-Thu	1P $39-129	2P/1B $39-129	2P/2B $39-129

XP $10; ages 17 and under stay free. Deposit required; handling fee imposed. Senior discount. AE, DI, DS, JC, VI. Gift shop. 3-4 stories; interior corridors. Roll-in showers. **Rooms:** 223. Movies, coffeemakers, refrigerators, ⊘. **Recreation:** Pool. **Services:** Airport transportation, laundry, business services. **Dining:** Restaurant.

TREASURE ISLAND AT THE MIRAGE   ♦♦♦ Resort Hotel
(702) 894-7444; FAX (702) 894-7446.
3½ mi S on the Strip; 3300 Las Vegas Bl S, 89109; Box 7711, 89193.

All year	1P $59-399	2P/1B $59-399	2P/2B $59-399

XP $25-50. Deposit required. AE, CB, DI, DS, JC, MC, VI. Gift shop. Pirate-themed resort; home to Cirque du Soleil. 36 stories; interior corridors. 🅰, 🎦. **Rooms:** 2891; 212 suites, $100-500 for up to 2 persons. Movies, VCRs, radios, data ports, ⊘; no cable TV. **Recreation:** Pool, massage, exercise room. **Services:** Valet parking, laundry, area transportation, business services. **Dining:** Restaurant; cocktail lounge; entertainment.

Restaurants

ANDIAMO   ♦♦♦ Regional Italian
(702) 732-5111.
In Las Vegas Hilton; 3000 Paradise Rd, 89109.
Dinner $20-30. AE, CB, DI, MC, VI. Open 6-11 pm. Casual attire. Comfortable and elegant surroundings; ⊘. Cocktail lounge. **Reservations:** Suggested. **Services:** Valet parking. **Menu:** Nice variety of dishes. A la carte.

ANDRE'S FRENCH RESTAURANT   ♦♦♦ French
(702) 385-5016.
At Lewis St and 401 S 6th St, 89101.
Dinner $20-44. AE, CB, DI, JC, MC, VI. Open 6 pm-11 pm. Closed major holidays. Semiformal attire. Country-French decor; several dining rooms; ⊘. Cocktail lounge. **Reservations:** Suggested. **Services:** Valet parking. **Menu:** Health-conscious menu items, a la carte.

ANTHONY'S FINE DINING   ♦♦♦ Continental
(702) 795-6000.
Exit I-15 at Tropicana; E 3 mi to 1550 E Tropicana Av, 89119.
Lunch $6-25, dinner $13-24. AE, DS, MC, VI. Open Sun-Fri 11 am-11 pm; Sat 5-11 pm. Closed major holidays. Semi-formal attire. Casual elegance with an Italian flair; ⊘. Cocktails. **Reservations:** Suggested. **Menu:** Early bird specials, a la carte.

BATTISTA'S HOLE IN THE WALL   ♦♦ Italian
(702) 732-1424.
I-15 exit Flamingo Rd E ³/₁₀ mi, 1 block E of The Strip; 4041 Audrie, 89109.
Dinner $16-30. AE, CB, DI, DS, MC, VI. Open daily 5 pm; Sun-Fri to 10:30 pm; Sat to 11 pm. Closed Thanksgiving, 12/25. Casual attire. Rustic decor; ⊘. Cocktail lounge. **Reservations:** Suggested. **Menu:** Dinners include house wine and cappuccino.

COUNTRY INN

♦♦ **American**
(702) 731-5035.

2 mi E of the Strip; 2425 E Desert Inn Rd, 89121.
Lunch and dinner $6-15. AE, CB, DI, DS, MC, VI. Open daily 7 am; Sun-Thu to 10 pm; Fri-Sat to 11 pm. Closed 12/25. Casual attire. Attractive country decor; casual atmosphere; ⊘. Beer and wine only. **Menu:** Children's menu, a la carte.

COUNTRY INN

♦♦ **American**
(702) 254-0520.

Exit I-15 Charleston, 4 mi W, S on Rainbow ³⁄₁₀ mi; 1401 S Rainbow, 89102.
Lunch $4-6, dinner $4-15. AE, CB, DI, DS, MC, VI. Open daily 7 am; Sun-Thu to 10 pm; Fri-Sat to 11 pm. Closed 12/25. Casual attire. Attractive country decor and friendly atmosphere; ⊘. Beer and wine only. **Reservations:** Suggested. **Menu:** Traditional dishes. Children's menu, a la carte.

GOLDEN STEER

♦♦ **Steakhouse**
(702) 384-4470.

Exit I-15 at Sahara, ³⁄₁₀ mi E, 1 block W of the Strip; 308 W Sahara Av, 89102.
Dinner $25-40. AE, CB, DI, MC, VI. Open 5 pm-11:30 pm. Closed Thanksgiving and 12/25. Semiformal attire; ⊘. Cocktail lounge. **Reservations:** Suggested. **Services:** Valet parking. **Menu:** Varied menu; chicken, veal and seafood. Italian specialties. A la carte.

KIEFER'S ATOP THE CARRIAGE HOUSE

♦♦♦ **Continental**
(702) 739-8000.

105 E Harmon, 89119.
Dinner $15-30. AE, CB, DI, DS, MC, VI. Open 7-10 am and 5-11 pm; Fri, Sat and Sun to midnight. Casual attire. ♿. Views of city, very romantic atmosphere; ⊘. Cocktail lounge minimum charge $5. **Reservations:** Suggested. **Menu:** A la carte.

MONTE CARLO RESTAURANT ⊛

♦♦♦♦ **French**
(702) 733-4444.

On the Strip in the Desert Inn; I-15 NB exit E Flamingo Av, SB exit E Sahara Av; at 3145 Las Vegas Bl S, 89109.
Dinner $65-105. AE, DI, DS, MC, VI. Open 6 pm-11 pm. Closed Tue & Wed. Semiformal attire. ♿. Long-established, service-oriented dining room, very intimate atmosphere. World class food and service; ⊘. Cocktail lounge. **Reservations:** Suggested. **Services:** Valet parking. **Menu:** A la carte.

PHILIPS SUPPER HOUSE

♦♦♦ **American**
(702) 873-5222.

2⅕ mi W of the Strip between Arville St and Decatur Bl; 4545 W Sahara Av, 89102.
Dinner $15-32. AE, CB, DI, DS, MC, VI. Open 4:30 pm-11 pm. Casual attire, ⊘. Cocktail lounge. **Reservations:** Suggested. **Menu:** Early bird specials. Prime eastern beef, seafood and Italian specialties.

YOLIE'S BRAZILIAN STEAK HOUSE

♦♦ **Brazilian**
(702) 794-0700.

On upper level of Citybank Park Plaza; 3900 Paradise Rd, Ste Z, 89109.
Lunch $7-13, dinner $15-44. AE, CB, DI, DS, MC, VI. Open Mon-Fri 11 am-3 and 5-11 pm; Sat-Sun from 5 pm. Closed 12/25. Casual attire. Informal atmosphere, ⊘. Cocktail lounge; entertainment. **Menu:** Variety of meats served from a skewer; also lamb, chicken and fish specialties. Children's menu, a la carte.

Laughlin

AVI HOTEL & CASINO ⓌⒶⒶ
◆◆◆ Hotel
(702) 535-5555; FAX (702) 535-5400.
9 mi S on Needles Hwy via Casino Dr; from I-40 exit W Broadway, 12 mi N at 10000 AHA Macav Pkwy; Box 77011, 89028-7011.

Fri-Sat	1P $65-70	2P/1B $65-70	2P/2B $65-70
Sun-Thu	1P $30-35	2P/1B $30-35	2P/2B $30-35

XP $5-9. 2-night minimum stay weekends. Package plans. Senior discount. AE, DI, DS, MC, VI. Beach. Gift shop. 4 stories; interior corridors. Roll-in showers. **Rooms:** 300. Movies, radios, refrigerators, ⊘. **Recreation:** Pool, whirlpool, swimming, marina, boat ramp, rental boats, wave runners, exercise room. **Services:** Laundry, business services. **Dining:** Dining room, $10-20; 24-hr coffee shop; deli; casino buffet, $6-8; cocktail lounge; entertainment.

BAYSHORE INN
◆ Motel
(702) 299-9010; FAX (702) 299-9194.
7 mi S of Davis Dam; 1955 W Casino Dr; Box 31377, 89029.

Fri-Sat	1P ...	2P/1B $55	2P/2B $55
Sun-Thu	1P $25	2P/1B $25	2P/2B $25

Maximum rates for up to 4 persons. DS, MC, VI. Pets. Central pool deck. 3 stories; interior corridors. **Rooms:** 98. ⊘. **Recreation:** Small pool. **Dining:** Restaurant nearby. Cocktail lounge.

COLORADO BELLE HOTEL & CASINO
◆◆ Hotel
(702) 298-4000; FAX (702) 299-0669.
3 mi S of Davis Dam; 2100 S Casino Dr; Box 77000, 89028.

Fri-Sat	1P $45-60	2P/1B $45-60	2P/2B $45-60
Sun-Thu	1P $21-39	2P/1B $39	2P/2B $39

Maximum rates for up to 4 persons. AE, CB, DI, DS, MC, VI. Gift shop. On the Colorado River, riverboat design. 6 stories; interior/exterior corridors. Roll-in showers, 🄩. **Rooms:** 1230. Shower baths, movies, safes, refrigerators, ⊘. **Recreation:** Pool. **Services:** Valet parking, business services. **Dining:** Restaurant; cocktail lounge; entertainment.

DON LAUGHLIN'S RIVERSIDE RESORT HOTEL & CASINO
◆◆◆ Hotel
(702) 298-2535; FAX (702) 298-2614.
2 mi S of Davis Dam, across river from Bullhead City, AZ; 1650 S Casino Wy; Box 500, 89029.

Fri-Sat	1P $49-109	2P/1B $49-109	2P/2B $49-109
Sun-Thu	1P $25- 71	2P/1B $25- 71	2P/2B $25- 71

Maximum rates for up to 4 persons. AE, CB, DI, DS, MC, VI. Pets. Gift shop. On the Colorado River. 26 stories; interior corridors. Roll-in showers, 🄩. **Rooms:** 1403; 9 whirlpool rooms. Combination/shower baths, movies, refrigerator, ⊘. **Recreation:** Pool. **Services:** Valet parking, business services. **Dining:** Restaurant; cocktails; entertainment.

EDGEWATER HOTEL/CASINO ⓌⒶⒶ
◆◆◆ Hotel
(702) 298-2453; FAX (702) 298-8165.
2⅛ mi S of Davis Dam; 2020 S Casino Dr; Box 77000, 89028.

Fri-Sat	1P $40-65	2P/1B $40-65	2P/2B $40-65
Sun-Thu	1P $21-38	2P/1B $21-38	2P/2B $21-38

Maximum rates for up to 4 persons. Deposit required; cancellation fee. AE, CB, DI, DS, MC, VI. Arcade. Southwestern decor. American Indian art. 3-26 stories; interior corridors. Roll-in showers, 🄩. **Rooms:** 1450. Combination/shower baths, movies, refrigerators, ⊘. **Recreation:** Pool, whirlpool. **Services:** Valet parking, laundry. **Dining:** Dining room; 2 restaurants $7-25; 24-hr coffee shop; deli; buffet $5; cocktail lounge; entertainment.

FLAMINGO HILTON LAUGHLIN

◆◆◆ Hotel
(702) 298-5111; FAX (702) 298-5129.

2 mi S of Davis Dam; 1900 S Casino Dr, 89029.

Fri-Sat	1P $55	2P/1B $55	2P/2B $55
Sun-Thu	1P $25	2P/1B $25	2P/2B $25

XP: $9; ages 12 and under stay free. AE, CB, DI, DS, JC, MC, VI. Gift shop. Spacious rooms. 18 stories; interior corridors. 🛗, 🖥. **Rooms:** 1912; suites $75-325 for up to 5 persons. River views, movies, radios, data ports, refrigerators, ⌀. **Recreation:** Pool, 3 lighted tennis courts, massage. **Services:** Laundry, business services. **Dining:** Restaurant; cocktail lounge; entertainment.

GOLDEN NUGGET LAUGHLIN

◆◆◆ Hotel
(702) 298-7111; FAX (702) 298-7122.

3⅛ mi S of Davis Dam; 2300 S Casino Dr; Box 77111, 89028.

Fri-Sat	1P $35-95	2P/1B $35-95	2P/2B $35-95
Sun-Thu	1P $21-65	2P/1B $21-65	2P/2B $21-65

XP $7. AE, DS, MC, VI. Gift shop. 30-foot glass-topped rain forest atrium with more than 500 tropical flora from around the world; tropical motif throughout. 4 stories; interior corridors. Roll-in showers, 🖥. **Rooms:** 300. Combination/shower baths, movies, radios, refrigerators, ⌀. **Recreation:** Pool. **Services:** Valet parking, laundry. **Dining:** Restaurant; cocktail lounge.

HARRAH'S CASINO HOTEL

◆◆◆ Hotel
(702) 298-4600; FAX (702) 298-6855.

5 mi S of Davis Dam, on the river; 2900 S Casino Dr, 89029.

Fri-Sat	1P $25-180	2P/1B $25-180	2P/2B $25-180
Sun-Thu	1P $25-140	2P/1B $25-140	2P/2B $25-140

XP $5. Deposit required; 3-day refund notice. AE, CB, DI, DS, MC, VI. Southwest architecture. On the Colorado River. 20 stories; exterior corridors. Roll-in showers. **Rooms:** 1600. Combination/shower baths, movies, radios, refrigerators, ⌀. **Recreation:** Pool, massage, exercise room. **Services:** Valet parking, laundry, business services. **Dining:** William Fisk's Steakhouse, see listing; cocktail lounge.

RAMADA EXPRESS HOTEL & CASINO

◆◆◆ Hotel
(702) 298-4200; FAX (702) 298-4619.

3 mi S of Davis Dam; 2121 S Casino Dr; Box 77771, 89028.

Fri-Sat	1P $54-89	2P/1B $54-89	2P/2B $54-89
Sun-Thu	1P $23-34	2P/1B $23-34	2P/2B $23-34

XP $5. Ages 18 and under stay free. AE, CB, DI, DS, MC, VI. Gift shop. 19th-century railroad motif; train ride. Adults-only tower. 24 stories; interior corridors. Roll-in showers, 🖥. **Rooms:** 1500. Combination/shower baths, movies, radios, data ports, coffeemakers, refrigerators, ⌀. **Recreation:** Pool, whirlpool. **Services:** Valet parking, laundry, business services. **Dining:** 3 restaurants $8-27; 24 hrs coffee shop; deli; buffet $5; casino; cocktail lounge.

Restaurant

WILLIAM FISK'S STEAKHOUSE

◆◆ American
(702) 298-6832.

In Harrah's Casino Hotel; 2900 S Casino Dr, 89029.

Dinner $15-25. AE, DI, DS, MC, VI. Open daily at 5 pm; Sun-Thu to 10 pm, Fri-Sat to 11 pm. Semiformal attire. Intimate dining atmosphere overlooking Colorado River; ⌀. Cocktails. **Reservations:** Suggested. **Services:** Valet parking. **Menu:** A la carte.

Primm

Lodging

PRIMM VALLEY RESORT & CASINO ᴀᴀᴀ

♦♦ Motor Inn

(702) 382-1212; FAX (702) 874-5195.
45 mi S of Las Vegas, E of and adjacent to I-15; State Line exit; Box 19119, Las Vegas 89019.

Fri	1P $45	2P/1B $45	2P/2B $45
Sat	1P $55	2P/1B $55	2P/2B $55
Sun-Thu	1P $25	2P/1B $25	2P/2B $25

XP $5; ages 12 and under stay free. 2-night minimum stay Fri-Sat. AE, DI, DS, MC, VI. Monorail. 4 stories; interior corridors. Roll-in showers. 🛆, Ç. **Rooms:** 660. Combination/shower baths, whirlpools, movies, coffeemakers, refrigerators, ⊘; no cable TV. **Recreation:** Pool (seasonal), whirlpool, putting green, 18-hole golf course, video game room, playground, ornamental Ferris wheel, carousel, bowling. **Services:** Valet parking, laundry, business services. **Dining:** Restaurant, $5-14; 24-hr buffet; coffee shop $4-5; cocktail lounge.

WHISKEY PETE'S HOTEL & CASINO

♦♦ Hotel

(702) 382-4388; FAX (702) 679-6606.
45 mi S of Las Vegas, W of and adjacent to I-15, State line exit; Box 19119, Las Vegas 89019-3718.

Fri	1P $33	2P/1B $33	2P/2B $33
Sat	1P $43	2P/1B $43	2P/2B $43
Sun-Thu	1P $25	2P/1B $25	2P/2B $25

XP $5; ages 17 and under stay free. 2-night minimum stay Fri-Sat. Deposit required. AE, DI, DS, MC, VI. Gift shop. 2-19 stories; interior corridors. **Rooms:** 777 rooms; suites, $75-200 for 2 persons; 12 whirlpool rooms. Combination/shower baths, movies, coffeemakers, ⊘; no cable TV. **Recreation:** Pool. **Services:** Valet parking, laundry, business services. **Dining:** Cocktail lounge; entertainment.

· Bullhead City, Arizona

Lodging

BEST WESTERN BULLHEAD CITY INN ᴀᴀᴀ

♦♦♦ Motel

(520) 754-3000; FAX (520) 754-5234.
1⅕ mi S of Laughlin Bridge on SR 95, then just E to 2360 4th St, 86429.

All year [CP]	1P $40-80	2P/1B $40-80	2P/2B $40-80

XP $5-10; ages 17 and under stay free. Deposit required. Weekly and monthly rates available. Senior discount. AE, CB, DI, DS, JC, MC, VI. Pets, $5 plus $25 deposit. Rooms decorated in light, contemporary colors. 2 stories; exterior corridors. **Rooms:** 88. Movies, refrigerators, microwaves, ⊘. **Recreation:** Pool, whirlpool. **Services:** Laundry, business services.

DAYS INN

♦♦ Motel

(520) 758-1711; FAX (520) 758-7937.
3½ mi S of Laughlin Bridge on SR 95, then just E; 2200 Rancho Colorado, 86442.

All year [CP]	1P $58	2P/1B $58	2P/2B $58

XP $5; ages 12 and under stay free. AE, CB, DI, DS, JC, MC, VI. Pets. Rooms are decorated in light colors. 3 stories; interior corridors. **Rooms:** 71; 7 1-bedroom suites, $53 for 2 persons. Combination/shower bathes, movies, refrigerators, microwaves, ⊘. **Recreation:** Pool. **Services:** Laundry.

LAKE MOHAVE RESORT 🆔   ◆ Resort Motor Inn
(520) 754-3245; FAX (520) 754-1125.
In the Lake Mead National Recreation Area at Katherine Landing, 3 mi N of SR 68 and Davis Dam, 86430.

All year	1P $60	2P/2B …	2P/2B $69

XP $6; ages 10 and under stay free. Deposit required; 3-day refund notice. DS, MC, VI. Pets $5. Rooms furnished in Western theme. 2 stories; exterior corridors; 14 efficiencies. **Rooms:** 52. Combination/shower baths, radios, coffeemaker, refrigerators; no cable TV. **Recreation:** Swimming, water-skiing, marina, boat ramp, rental boats, houseboats, fishing. **Dining:** Restaurant at Lake Mohave, across from establishment; daily at 8 am, Mon-Thu to 8 pm; Fri-Sat to 9 pm; $9-14; cocktails.

LODGE ON THE RIVER   ◆◆ Motel
(520) 758-8080; FAX (520) 758-8283.
3⅗ mi S of Laughlin Bridge on SR 95; 1717 Hwy 95, 86442.

All year	1P $26	2P/1B $31	2P/2B $35

XP $5; ages 12 and under stay free. AE, CB, DI, DS, MC, VI. Pets. At the Colorado River; contemporary-style rooms decorated in light colors. 2 stories; exterior corridors. **Rooms:** 64; 13 riverfront suites with microwave, refrigerator and balcony, $59-95 for 2 persons. Combination/shower baths, coffeemakers, refrigerators, microwaves, ∅. **Recreation:** Pool. **Services:** Laundry.

SUNRIDGE HOTEL & CONFERENCE CENTER 🆔   ◆◆◆ Motor Inn
(520) 754-4700; FAX (520) 754-1225.
3 mi N on SR 95, 1³⁄₁₀ mi E on SR 68 at 839 Landon Dr, 86429.

All Year [CP]	1P $49-79	2P/1B $49-79	2P/2B $49-79

XP $5; ages 18 and under stay free. Weekly rates. Senior discount. AE, CB, DI, DS, MC, VI. Small pets, $50 deposit. On quiet hillside off highway. 4 stories; exterior corridors. **Rooms:** 148. Radios, refrigerators, microwaves, ∅. **Recreation:** Pool, exercise room. **Services:** Laundry, business services.

TRAVELODGE GRAND VISTA   ◆◆ Motel
(520) 763-3300; FAX (520) 763-4447.
2 mi N on SR 95, then just E at 1817 Arcadia Plaza, 86442.

Fri-Sat	1P $65	2P/1B $65	2P/2B $65
Sun-Thu	1P $49	2P/1B $49	2P/2B $49

Deposit required. AE, CB, DI, DS, MC, VI. On a bluff with a view of the Colorado River. 3 stories; interior corridors. **Rooms:** 80. Movies, coffeemakers, refrigerators, microwaves, ∅. **Recreation:** Pool. **Services:** Business services. **Dining:** Restaurant nearby.

Restaurant

TOWNE'S SQUARE CAFE   ◆◆ American
(520) 763-2477.
3⅗ mi S of Laughlin Bridge on SR 95, 1751 W Hwy 95, Ste 25, 86442.
Lunch $5-7; dinner $7-12. AE, DI, DS, MC, VI. Open 6 am-10:30 pm. Closed 12/25. Casual attire. Nice family-style restaurant with homey decor and atmosphere; ∅. Beer and wine only. **Services:** Carryout. **Menu:** Good selection of sandwiches, beef, chicken and seafood entrees. Children's menu, seniors' menu, health-conscious menu.

Campgrounds & Trailer Parks

*Warm weather, and nearby scenic and recreation areas attract thousands of campers to Las Vegas and Laughlin every year. Camping accommodations range from simple RV lots located close to the gambling action and glitz to more rugged settings in surrounding areas, including Bullhead City, Arizona. The campgrounds in this section are listed alphabetically by city or closest recreation area—**Boulder City**, **Lake Mead National Recreation Area (Lake Mead** and **Lake Mohave)**, **Las Vegas**, **Primm**, **Red Rock Canyon National Conservation Area**, **Spring Mountains National Recreation Area**, **Valley of Fire State Park** and **Bullhead City, Arizona**. Unless otherwise noted, campgrounds are open all year.*

*T*he following listings show the nightly camping fee for the number of people specified, include a recreational vehicle or automobile (with or without a trailer). Electricity, water and sewer RV hookups are indicated by the letters **E**, **W** and **S**, respectively.

Private campgrounds have been inspected by an Auto Club representative and meet AAA requirements for recommendation. Private campgrounds that did not meet the requirements for listing or that were not inspected have not been included in this book.

Public campgrounds typically allow a more natural experience or have fewer services, and as a result usually do not meet AAA requirements for recommendation; they are listed here as a service. Information for the public campgrounds was obtained from the administering government agency, which is shown at the end of the individual listings, i.e., National Forest (NF); National Park Service (NPS); Bureau of Land Management (BLM); State; County; and Private.

The maximum stay for camping in the Lake Mead National Recreation Area is 30 consecutive days, with a cumulative total of 90 camping days in a consecutive 12-month period; the Spring

Mountain National Recreation Area, as well as BLM campsites, have set camping limits to a maximum of 14 consecutive days in any 30-day period.

The ⓐⓐⓐ in a private campground listing identifies the establishment as a AAA Official Appointment; it indicates that the campground has expressed a particular interest in serving AAA members. In order to communicate this desire to the traveling public, these facilities have purchased the right to display the AAA emblem.

Bringing the family pet? Pets on leashes are welcome in most campgrounds. Leashes should be no longer than 6 feet. Be aware that some campgrounds charge a nominal fee for pets (these are noted).

For an additional fee, an RV towing and tire-change service option is available for motor homes, campers and travel/camping trailers. Call (800) AAA-HELP; hearing impaired call (800) 955-4TDD.

Reservations

Campsites that can be reserved by phoning the campground or administering agency directly indicate "reservations" or "deposit required." Any other reservation system is outlined; otherwise, camping is "first come, first served."

One toll-free call will connect you to the National Recreation Reservation Service (NRRS), a reservation system used by the Army Corps of Engineers and the National Forest Service. Reservations may be made daily 10 a.m. to 7 p.m. EST by calling the toll-free numbers (877) 444-6777 or (877) 833-6777 (TDD). Campgrounds where reservations are accepted may be reserved up to 240 days in advance, and an $8.65 reservation fee applies. The reservation center accepts both MasterCard and VISA. After a reservation is made, there is a $10 fee to change or to cancel a reservation. Campers who cancel after 6 p.m. on the day of their arrival will be charged the $10 cancellation fee and face forfei-

ture of their first night's camping fee; campsites will be held for 24 hours, after which those who do not show or those who cancel will be assessed a $20 fee in addition to the forfeiture of the first night's camping fee.

Additional fees may be charged for some services and facilities, such as showers, laundry, and recreational activities or equipment. Swimming pools may or may not be heated.

Where accepted, major credit cards honored by the campgrounds appear in each listing and are abbreviated as follows: AE=American Express, CB=Carte Blanche, DI=Diners Club, DS=Discover, JC=Japanese Credit Bureau, MC=MasterCard, VI=VISA.

ALL CAMPING FEES ARE SUBJECT TO CHANGE.

Boulder City

BOULDER OAKS RV RESORT   *(702) 294-4425; FAX (702) 294-4426.*
1010 Industrial Rd, 89005.
All year $23 for 2
XP $5. Deposit required; handling fee. DS, MC, VI. Pets. Some sites with view of distant Lake Mead. Disposal station. **Sites:** 275 RV. 275 EWS; 50 amps. Cable TV and phone hookups. **Recreation:** Pool, sauna, whirlpool, recreation room. **Services:** Laundry, groceries. (Private)

Lake Mead National Recreation Area

LAKE MEAD NATIONAL RECREATION
AREA HEADQUARTERS   *(702) 293-8990, 293-8907.*
25 mi SE of Las Vegas; 601 Nevada Hwy, Boulder City, 89005.

Lake Mead

BOULDER BEACH   *(702) 293-8907.*
6 mi NE of Boulder City on SR 166.
All year $10 for 8
First come, first served. Pets. Disposal station, flush toilets, grills, picnic tables. **Sites:** 142 tent/RV. **Recreation:** Boats, boat ramp. **Services:** Laundry, groceries. (NPS)

Katherine Landing, on Lake Mohave, has full marina services in addition to camping facilities.

CALLVILLE BAY *(702) 293-8907.*
22 mi NE of Henderson on SR 147/167.
All year $10 for 8
First come, first served. Pets. Disposal station, flush toilets, grills, picnic tables. **Sites:** 80 tent/RV. **Recreation:** Boats, boat ramp. **Services:** Laundry. (NPS)

ECHO BAY *(702) 293-8907.*
30 mi S of Overton on SR 167.
All year $10 for 8
First come, first served. Pets. Disposal station, flush toilets, grills, picnic tables. **Sites:** 155 tent/RV. **Recreation:** Boats, boat ramp. **Services:** Laundry. (NPS)

LAS VEGAS BAY *(702) 293-8907.*
8 mi NE of Henderson or 13 mi NW of Boulder City on SR 166.
All year $10 for 8
First come, first served. Pets. Disposal station, flush toilets, grills, picnic tables. **Sites:** 86 tent/RV. **Recreation:** Boats, boat ramp. (NPS)

TEMPLE BAR *(702) 293-8907.*
26 mi E of Boulder City on US 93 then 28 mi N on Temple Bar access road.
All year $10 for 8
First come, first served. Pets. Disposal station, flush toilets, grills, picnic tables. **Sites:** 166 tent/RV. **Recreation:** Marina, boats, boat ramp, boat and auto fuel. **Services:** Laundry, groceries. (NPS)

Lake Mohave

COTTONWOOD COVE *(702) 293-8907.*
14 mi E of Searchlight on US 95.
All year $10 for 8
First come, first served. Pets. Disposal station, flush toilets, grills, picnic tables. **Sites:** 145 tent/RV. **Recreation:** Boats, boat ramp. **Services:** Laundry, groceries. (NPS)

COTTONWOOD COVE RV PARK & MARINA 🚐 *(702) 297-1464.*
Between Las Vegas and Needles; 14 mi E of Searchlight, off US 95 at Lake Mohave; Box 1000, 89046.
All year $17 for 8
Air conditioning, $3. Check-out 10 am. AE, DS, MC, VI. Pets. Desert landscape. Disposal station, piped water, flush toilets, showers. **Sites:** 73 RV. 73 EWS. **Recreation:** Beach, swimming, fishing, boat ramp, marina, houseboats, powerboats, water-skiing and equipment. **Services:** Laundry, groceries, propane. **Dining:** Snack bar. (Private)

KATHERINE *(702) 293-8907; (520) 754-3272.*
6 mi N of Bullhead City, off US 95/SR 68.
All year $10 for 8
First come, first served. 30-day stay limit. Disposal station, flush toilets, grills, picnic tables. **Sites:** 162 tent/RV. **Recreation:** Boats, boat ramp; fishing, swimming. **Services:** Laundry. (NPS)

Las Vegas

BOULDER LAKES RV RESORT 🚐 *(702) 435-1157; FAX (702) 435-1125.*
1 mi E of I-515/SR 93 and 95, exit Russell Rd, ¼ mi N at Desert Horizons Rd; 6201 Boulder Hwy, 89122.

RV camping facilities in Las Vegas generally feature swimming pools, recreation rooms and convenient access to casino entertainment.

All year $20-25 for 2
XP $2. Weekly and monthly rates available. MC, VI. Desert atmosphere, paved roads and pads. Flush toilets. **Sites:** 417 RV; 50-ft maximum RV length. 417 EWS. Cable TV and phone hookups. **Recreation:** Pool, saunas, whirlpools, recreation room. **Services:** Laundry, groceries. (Private)

CIRCUSLAND RV PARK
(702) 794-3757; FAX (702) 792-2280.
2⅛ mi S on the Strip, adjacent to Circus Circus Hotel & Casino; 500 Circus Circus Dr, 89109.
All year $17-25 for 8
Deposit required. Senior discount. AE, CB, DI, DS, JC, MC, VI. Pets. Disposal station, flush toilets. **Sites:** 399 RV. 399 EWS. All paved sites; many pull-thru. **Recreation:** Pool, sauna, whirlpool, playground. **Services:** Laundry, groceries. (Private)

DESERT OASIS LAS VEGAS RV RESORT
(702) 260-2020; FAX (702) 263-5160.
Exit I-15 at Blue Diamond Rd (Exit 33), ½ mi E to Las Vegas Bl, ½ mi S to 2711 W Windmill, 89123.
5/1-9/30 $19-46.58 for 2
10/1-4/30 $23.50-51.50 for 2
DS, MC, VI. Small pets. Disposal station, lounge, flush toilets. **Sites:** 702 RV. 702 EWS. Cable TV and phone hookups. **Recreation:** Pools, whirlpool, recreation room, fully equipped exercise facility, 18-hole putting course on natural turf greens. **Services:** Laundry, groceries, propane. (Private)

LAS VEGAS RESORT KOA
(702) 451-5527; FAX (702) 434-8729.
4 mi SE on US 93 and 95, just S of Desert Inn Rd; 4315 Boulder Hwy, 89121.
All year $23.95-29.95 for 2
XP $3-5. Deposit required; monthly rates. DS, MC, VI. Pets. Disposal station, flush toilets. **Sites:** 240 RV, many pull-thru; 60 tent sites. 240 EW, 180 S. **Recreation:** Pool, wading pool, whirlpool (open 5/15-9/15), sports court, recreation room, playground. **Services:** Laundry, area transportation to Strip, groceries, propane, self-service RV and car wash. (Private)

SAM'S TOWN RV PARKS ⊛
(702) 454-8055; FAX (702) 454-8014.
1 mi E of I-515/US 93 and 95, Flamingo exit; 5225 Boulder Hwy, 89122.
All year $18-20 for 2
14-night stay limit. Deposit required. AE, CB, DI, DS, MC, VI. Pets. Attractive grounds. Disposal station, flush toilets. **Sites:** 500 RV. 460 EWS. Some pull-thru sites. No tents allowed. **Recreation:** Pools, whirlpools, recreation room. **Services:** Laundry. (Private)

SILVERTON RV RESORT ⊛
(702) 263-7777; FAX (702) 897-4208.
4995 Boulder Hwy, 89121.
Fri-Sat $20 for 8
Sun-Thu $18 for 8
Deposit required. AE, CB, DI, DS, MC, VI. Small pets. Disposal station, flush toilets, **Sites:** 460 RV; 60-ft maximum RV length. 239 EWS; 50 amps. Cable TV and phone hookups. **Recreation:** Pool, sauna, recreation room, sports court. **Services:** Laundry, groceries. (Private)

SUNRISE RESORT & RV PARK
(702) 458-7275; FAX (702) 898-7275.
4445 Boulder Hwy, 89121.
All year $19 for 4
Deposit required. AE, DS, MC, VI. Small pets. Flush toilets. **Sites:** 239 RV. 239 EWS; 50 amps. Cable TV and phone hookups. **Recreation:** Pool, whirlpool, putting green, exercise room, recreation room, pool table. **Services:** Laundry, groceries, propane. (Private)

Primm

PRIMADONNA RV VILLAGE Ⓢ   *(702) 382-1212; FAX (702) 679-5494.*
E of I-15, Primm exit, 45 mi S of Las Vegas; Box 19119, Primm 89019.
All year $12 for 8
56-night maximum stay. AE, DI, DS, MC, VI. Pets. Disposal station, piped water, flush toilets. **Sites:** 200 tent/RV. 200 EWS. Most pull-thru sites. Cable TV hookups. **Recreation:** Pool, whirlpool, playground, recreation room, sports court. **Services:** Laundry, area transportation to casino, groceries, propane. (Private)

Red Rock Canyon National Conservation Area

LAS VEGAS FIELD OFFICE   *(702) 647-5000.*
BLM, 4765 W Vegas Dr, Las Vegas, 89108.

Red Rock Canyon Visitor Center   *(702) 363-1921.*
1000 Scenic Dr, Las Vegas, 89124; mail: Bureau of Land Management, HCR-33 Box 5500, Las Vegas, 89124.

13-Mile Campground
At the 13-mile marker on SR 159/W Charleston Bl.
All year $10 for 10 (RVs), $5 for 5 (tents)
First come, first served. Pets, $3. El 3100. Primitive toilets, picnic tables, barbecue pits, no showers. Visitor center 2 mi W of campground. **Sites:** 15 tent, 57 tent/RV sites. (BLM)

Spring Mountains National Recreation Area

HEADQUARTERS   *(702) 873-8800.*
Humboldt-Toiyabe National Forest, 2881 S Valley View, Ste 16, Las Vegas, 89102.

Spring Mountains National Recreation Area
35 mi NW of Las Vegas within the Humboldt-Toiyabe National Forest via US 95, turn off at SR 157/Kyle Canyon Rd or SR 156/Lee Canyon Rd. Campgrounds open daily May through Sep; early and late season may vary due to the weather. For campsite reservations, call the NRRS. Unless indicated, the maximum RV length is 30 ft.

Dolomite
43 mi from Las Vegas in Lee Canyon on SR 156.
All year $13 per family
$4 per additional vehicle. NRRS. Pets. El 8400. Piped water, flush and primitive toilets, barbecues, fire rings, picnic tables, no showers. **Sites:** 30 tent/RV. **Recreation:** Nature trails. (NF)

Fletcher View
34½ mi from Las Vegas in Kyle Canyon on SR 157.
All year $13 per family
First come, first served. El 7200. Piped water, primitive toilets, barbecues, fire rings, some picnic tables, no showers. **Sites:** 11 tent/RV; 25-ft maximum RV length. **Recreation:** Riding stable within 1 mile. (NF)

Hilltop
15 mi NW on US 95, 17 mi W on SR 157, 6 mi NW on SR 158.
All year $13 per family
Due to short parking spurs and a narrow approach road, this campground is not recommended for trailers and motor homes. NRRS. El 8400. Piped water, flush toilets, showers, barbecues, fire rings, picnic tables. **Sites:** 31 tent/RV. 2 units are wheelchair accessible. **Recreation:** Nature trails. (NF)

Kyle Canyon
15 mi NW on US 95, 17½ mi W on SR 157.
All year $13 per family
NRRS. El 7000. Piped water, primitive toilets, barbecues, fire rings, picnic tables; no showers. **Sites:** 19 tent/RV sites. 10 units are wheelchair accessible. **Recreation:** Riding stable within 1 mile. (NF)

McWilliams
In Lee Canyon, 43 mi from Las Vegas in Lee Canyon on SR 156.
All year $13 per family
NRRS. El 8400. Piped water, flush and primitive toilets, barbecues, fire rings, picnic tables, no showers. **Sites:** 31 tent/RV. **Recreation:** Horseshoe pit. (NF)

Valley of Fire State Park

VALLEY OF FIRE STATE PARK VISITOR CENTER *(702) 397-2088.*
50 mi NE of Las Vegas via I-15 and SR 169; Box 515, Overton, 89040.

Valley of Fire Campgrounds
There are 2 campgrounds in the park located less than ½ mi apart. As of press time, one campground was closed due to flood damage and a reopening date had not been established. The data below reflects the diminished capacity of the camping facilities. Individuals are encouraged to call in order to verify information.
All year $12 for 8
First come, first served. Pets. Visitor center. Piped water, flush and primitive toilets, showers, barbecues, fire rings, picnic tables. **Sites:** 3 tent sites; 19 tent/RV sites total. 2 sites are wheelchair accessible. **Recreation:** Nature trail. (State)

Bullhead City, Arizona

MOHAVE COUNTY PARKS-DAVIS CAMP *(520) 754-4606.*
1 mi N on SR 95, below Davis Dam.
All year $8-15 for 4
14-night stay limit on beach. First come, first served. MC, VI. Pets; dogs, $1 per day. El 520. On Colorado River. Disposal station, piped water, flush toilets, showers, barbecues, fire rings. **Sites:** 171 RV; 50-ft maximum RV length. 141 EWS, 30 WE. Wheelchair accessible. **Recreation:** Swimming, fishing, boating, boat ramp, dock, playground. **Services:** Laundry, groceries (within 5 miles), propane. (County)

SNOWBIRD RV RESORT *(520) 768-7141.*
8 mi S on SR 95, just E on Joy Ln, 1600 Joy Ln, 86426.
All year $16 for 2
XP $1-3. Pets. Disposal station, piped water, flush toilets. 9-hole golf course, complimentary to guests. **Sites:** 10 tent, 125 RV. 125 EWS; 50 amps. Cable TV and phone hookups. Washer/dryer hookups, $3. **Recreation:** Pool, whirlpool, recreation room, playground. (Private)

Index

This index contains listings for points of interest, recreational activities, events and services.

Index to Advertisers

For information about placing an advertisement in
Automobile Club of Southern California publications, please contact:

Acknowledgements

Writer	Mark Chiaramonte
Cartographer	Andrew M. Gordon
Graphic Artist	Michael C. Lee
Editor	Kristine Miller

Photography

6, 15 (archive), 38, 51, 55, 57, 59, 73, 79 (dam), 91, 96, 103	**Las Vegas News Bureau**
(Cover), 5, 34, 36, 39 (Lied Museum), 42, 46, 67, 72, 98	**Todd Masinter**
9, 15 (petroglyphs), 16, 41, 49, 61, 68, 79 (dock), 95	**David J. Brackney**
13, 23, 65, 72, 75, 84, 85	**Robert Brown**
11, 70, 138	**Chris Hart**
139	**Circus Circus Hotel & Casino**
26	**Ethel M Chocolates Factory**
54	**Excalibur Hotel & Casino**
53	**Flamingo Hilton**
21	**Las Vegas Wedding Coordinators**
39 (pianos)	**Liberace Museum**
104	**McCarran International Airport**
43	**Scandia Family Fun Center**
45	**Wet 'n Wild**
10	**World of Coca-Cola Las Vegas**

Notes

Notes

Notes